ORDINARY PEOPLE CHANGE THE WORLD

I am George Washington

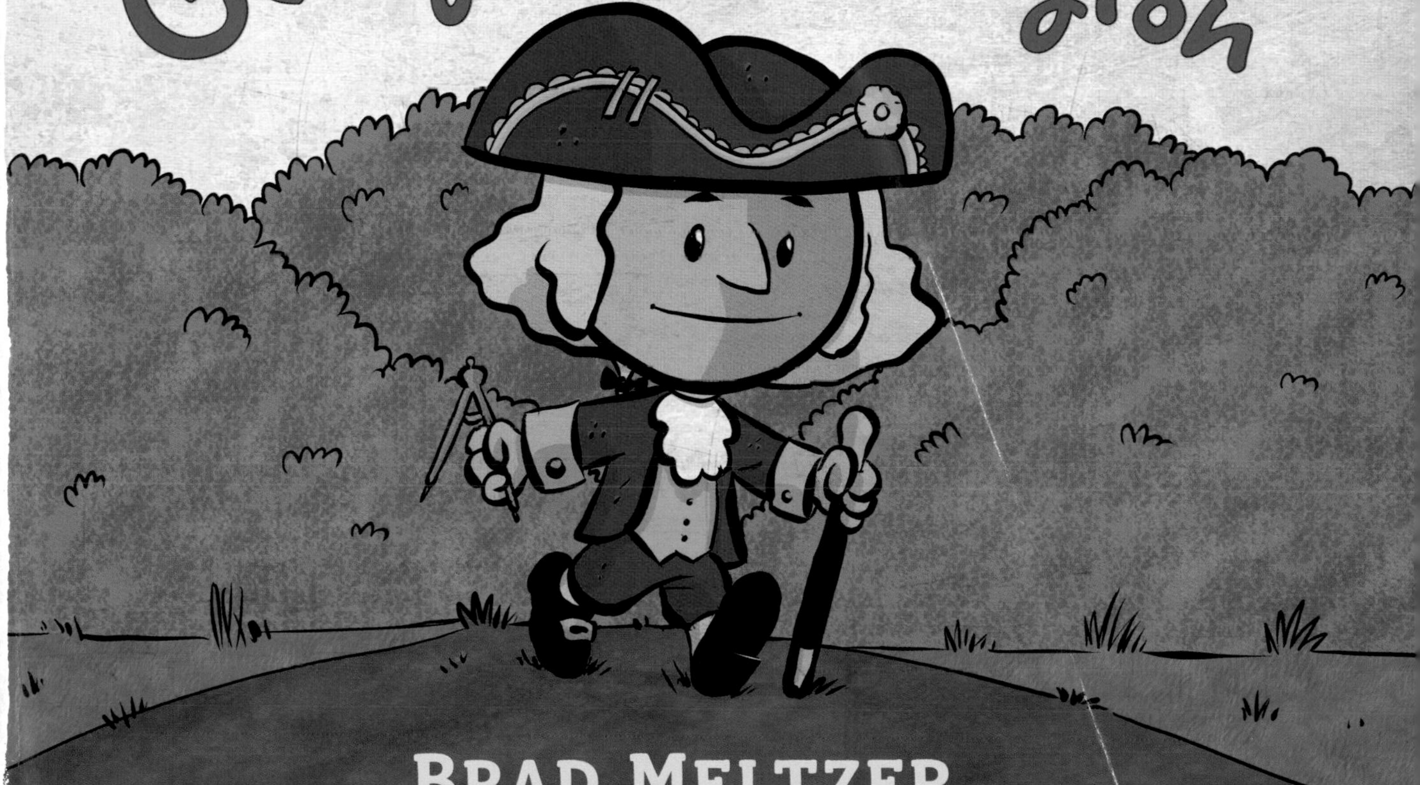

BRAD MELTZER
illustrated by Christopher Eliopoulos

ROCKY POND BOOKS

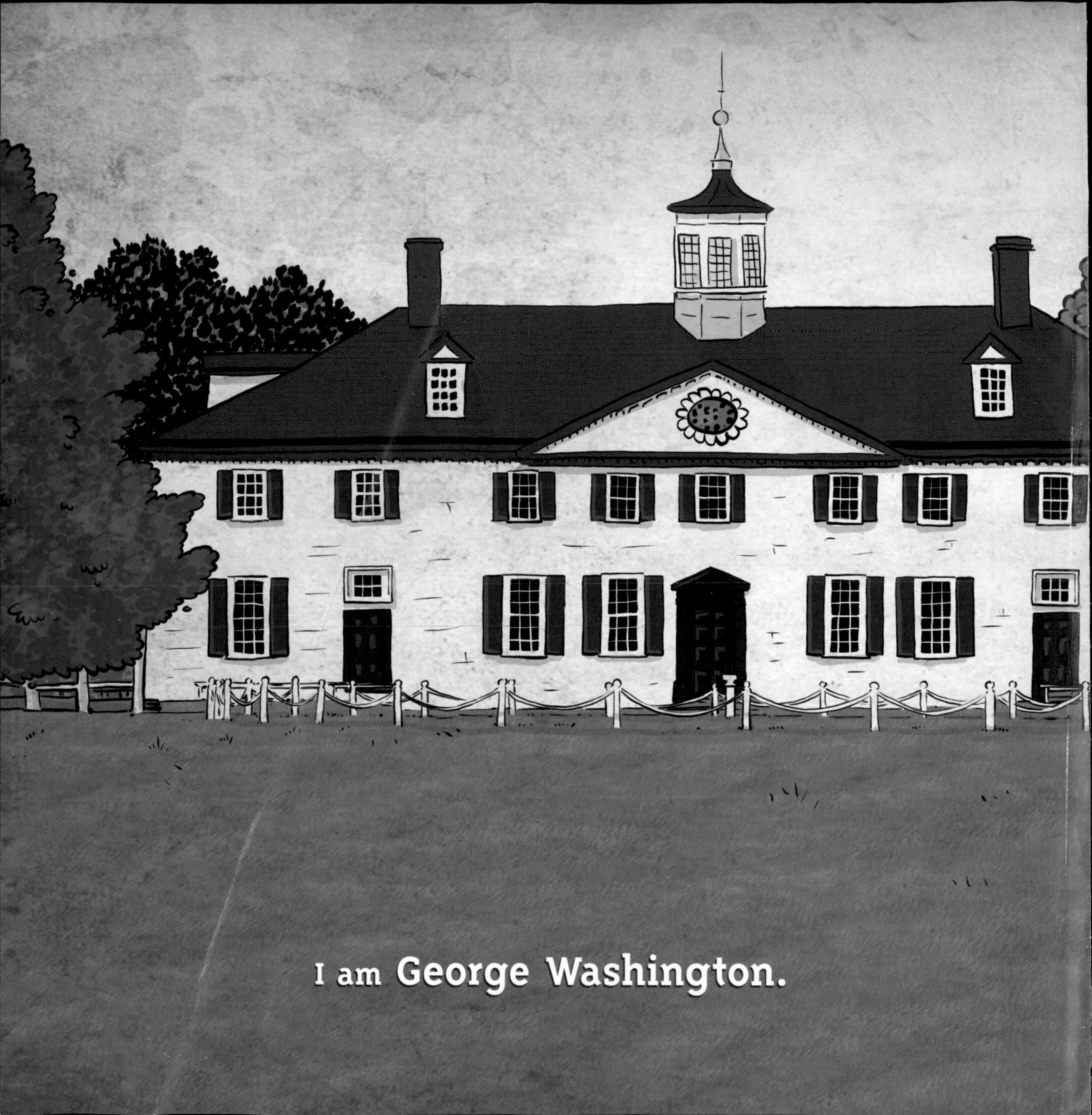

I am **George Washington.**

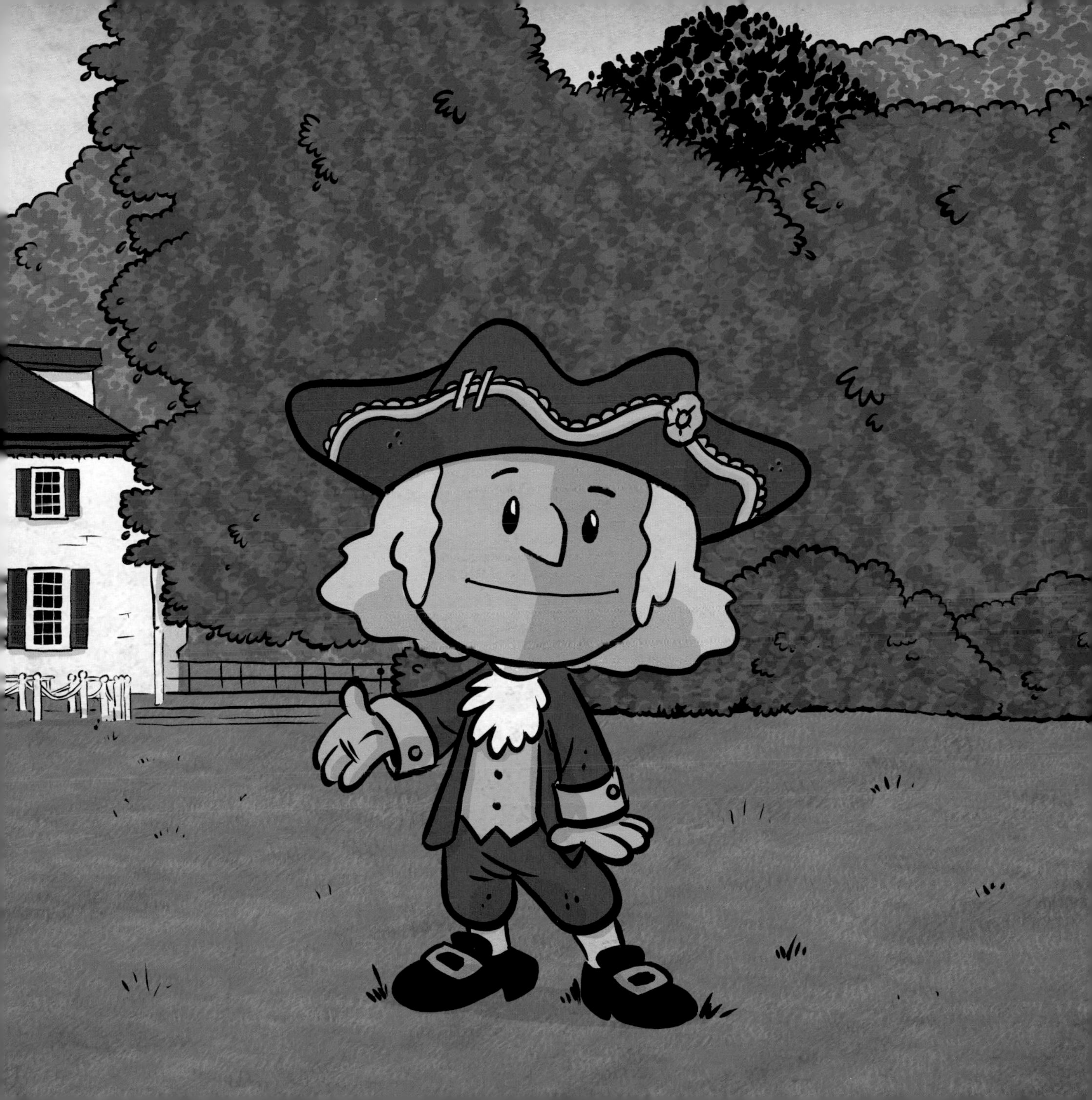

You know what one of the hardest things in life is?

Being the first.

When you're the first to try something new, there's no one to show you the way.

But when I was little, I wasn't the first. I was the fourth of nine children.

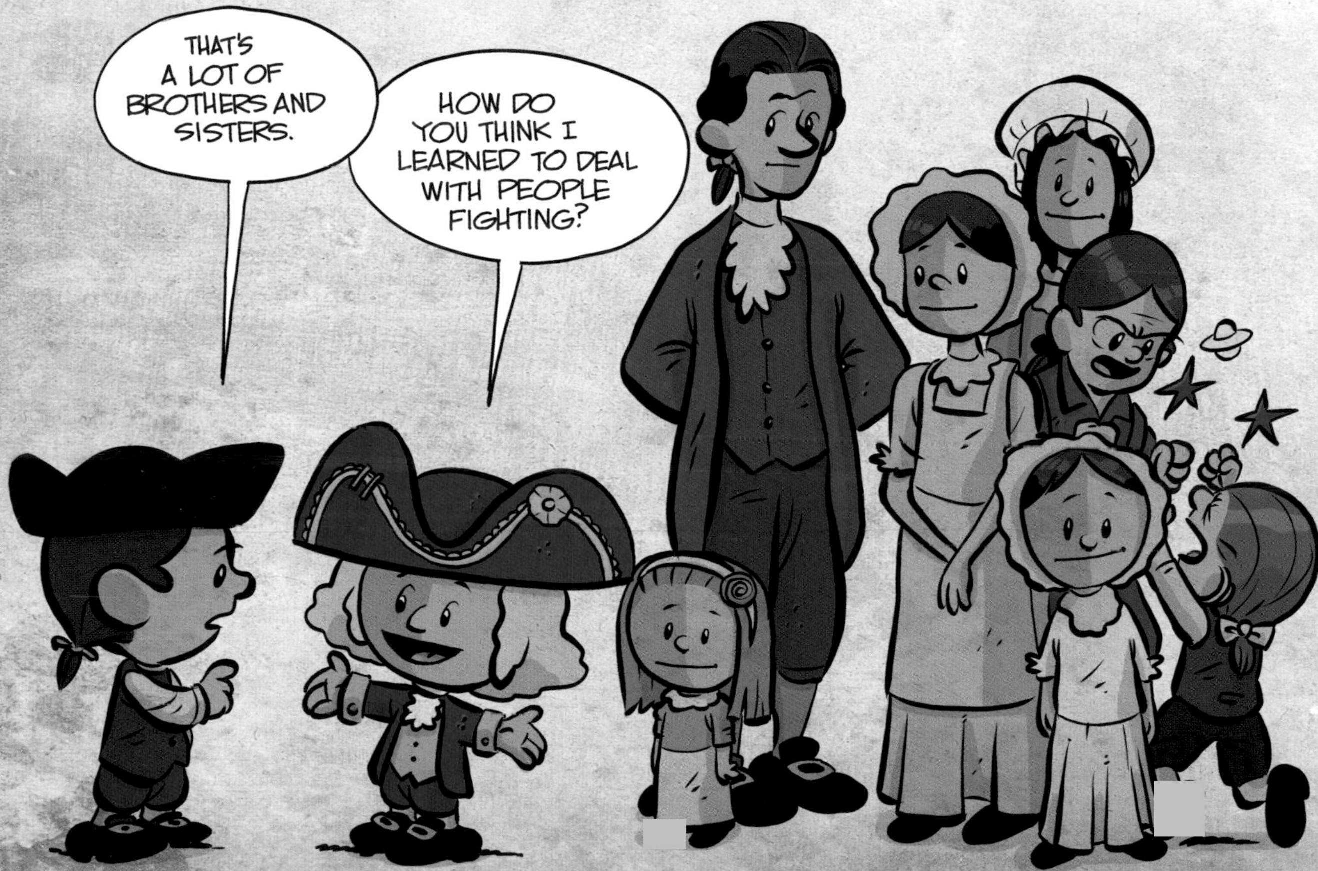
THAT'S A LOT OF BROTHERS AND SISTERS.
HOW DO YOU THINK I LEARNED TO DEAL WITH PEOPLE FIGHTING?

When I was *really* little, I lived at a place called Mount Vernon, which had a huge river running through the backyard and unexplored forests in every direction.

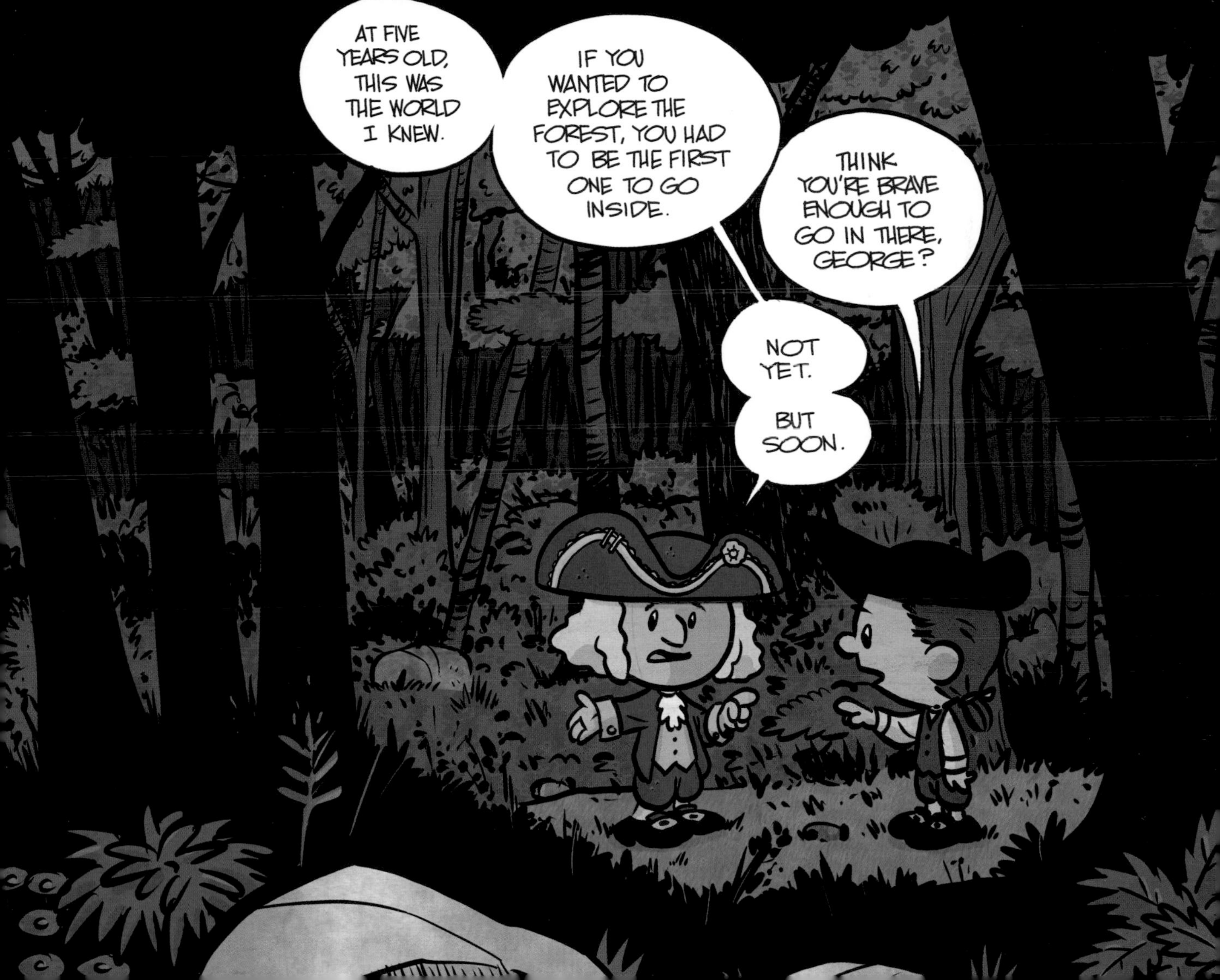
AT FIVE YEARS OLD, THIS WAS THE WORLD I KNEW.
IF YOU WANTED TO EXPLORE THE FOREST, YOU HAD TO BE THE FIRST ONE TO GO INSIDE.
THINK YOU'RE BRAVE ENOUGH TO GO IN THERE, GEORGE?
NOT YET.
BUT SOON.

People will tell you that I was a perfect boy.

They'll say I didn't tell a lie after I chopped down a cherry tree.

But that cherry tree story isn't true.

Like most boys back then, I liked swimming . . .

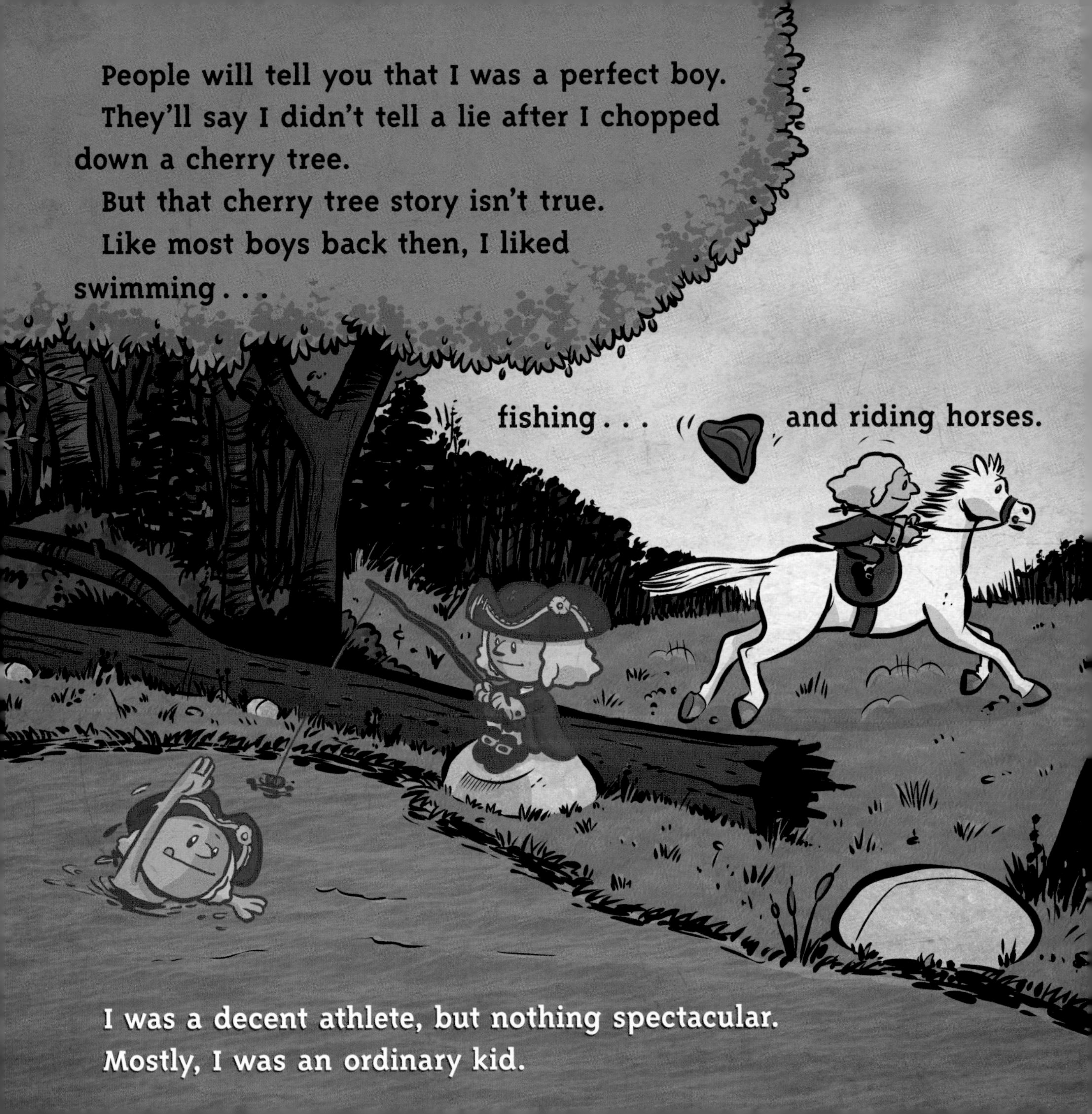

fishing . . . and riding horses.

I was a decent athlete, but nothing spectacular.
Mostly, I was an ordinary kid.

I liked books, and even liked to dance. I was great at it.

In school, my best subject was math. I was pretty good at writing, but I was always a terrible speller.

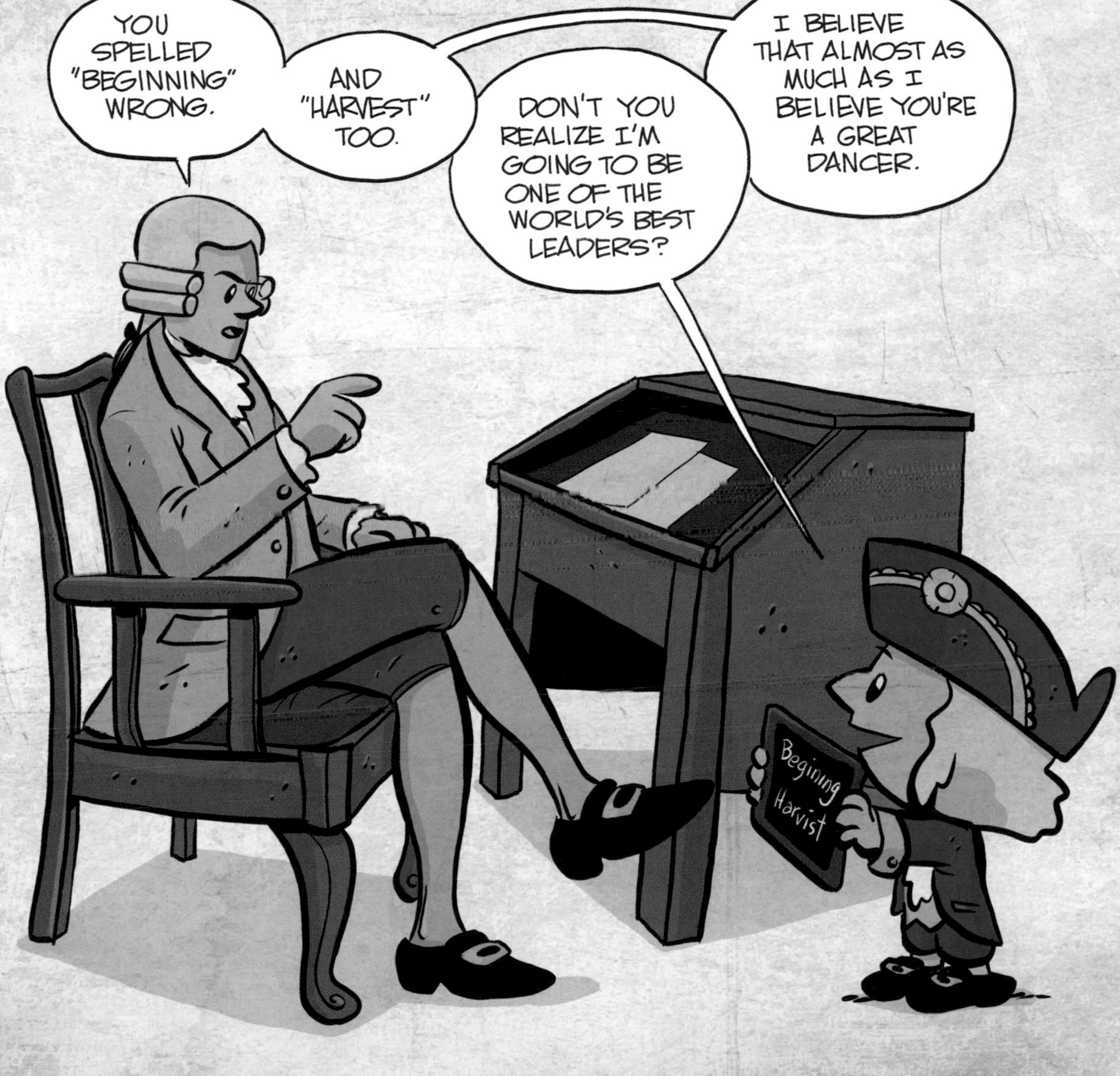
YOU SPELLED "BEGINNING" WRONG.
AND "HARVEST" TOO.
DON'T YOU REALIZE I'M GOING TO BE ONE OF THE WORLD'S BEST LEADERS?
I BELIEVE THAT ALMOST AS MUCH AS I BELIEVE YOU'RE A GREAT DANCER.
Begining
Harvist

But remember when I said that it's hard to be the first?
It's easier when there's someone showing you how it's done.

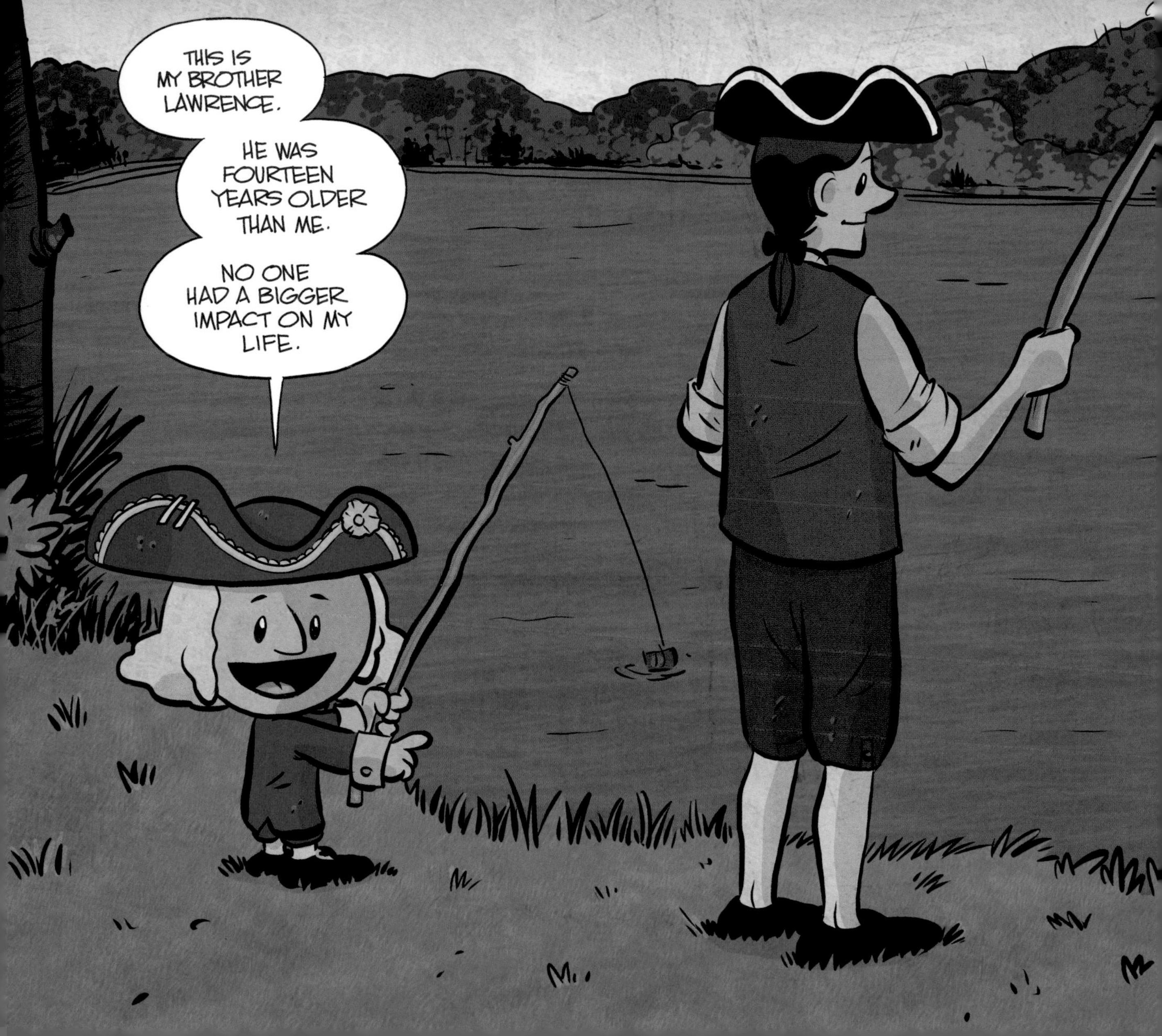
THIS IS MY BROTHER LAWRENCE.
HE WAS FOURTEEN YEARS OLDER THAN ME.
NO ONE HAD A BIGGER IMPACT ON MY LIFE.

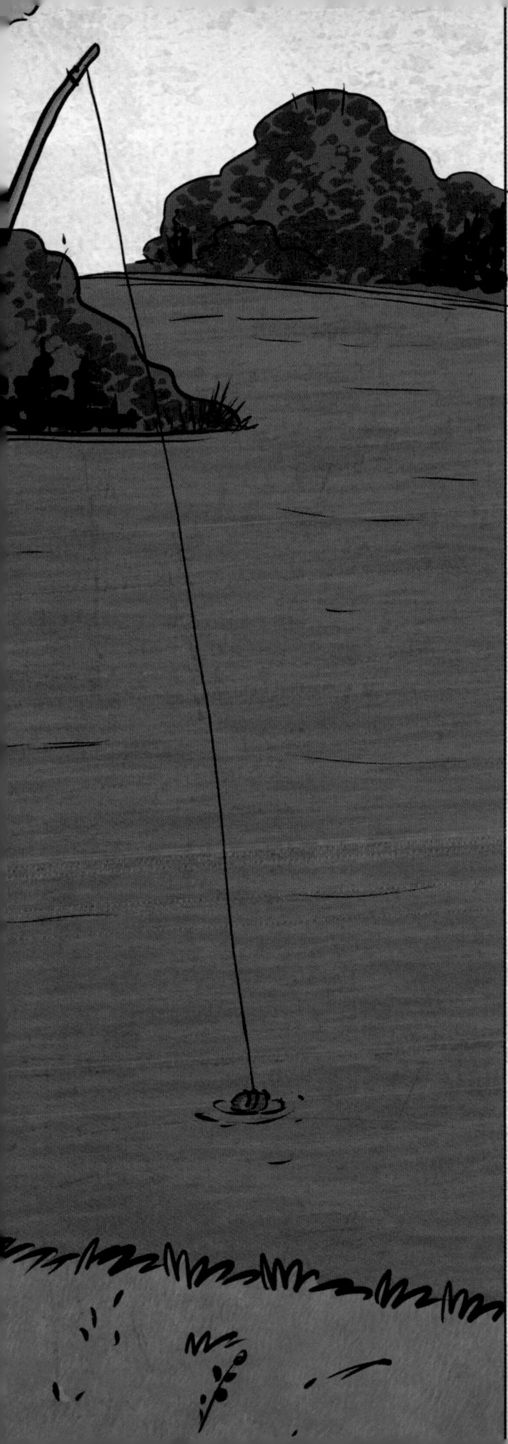

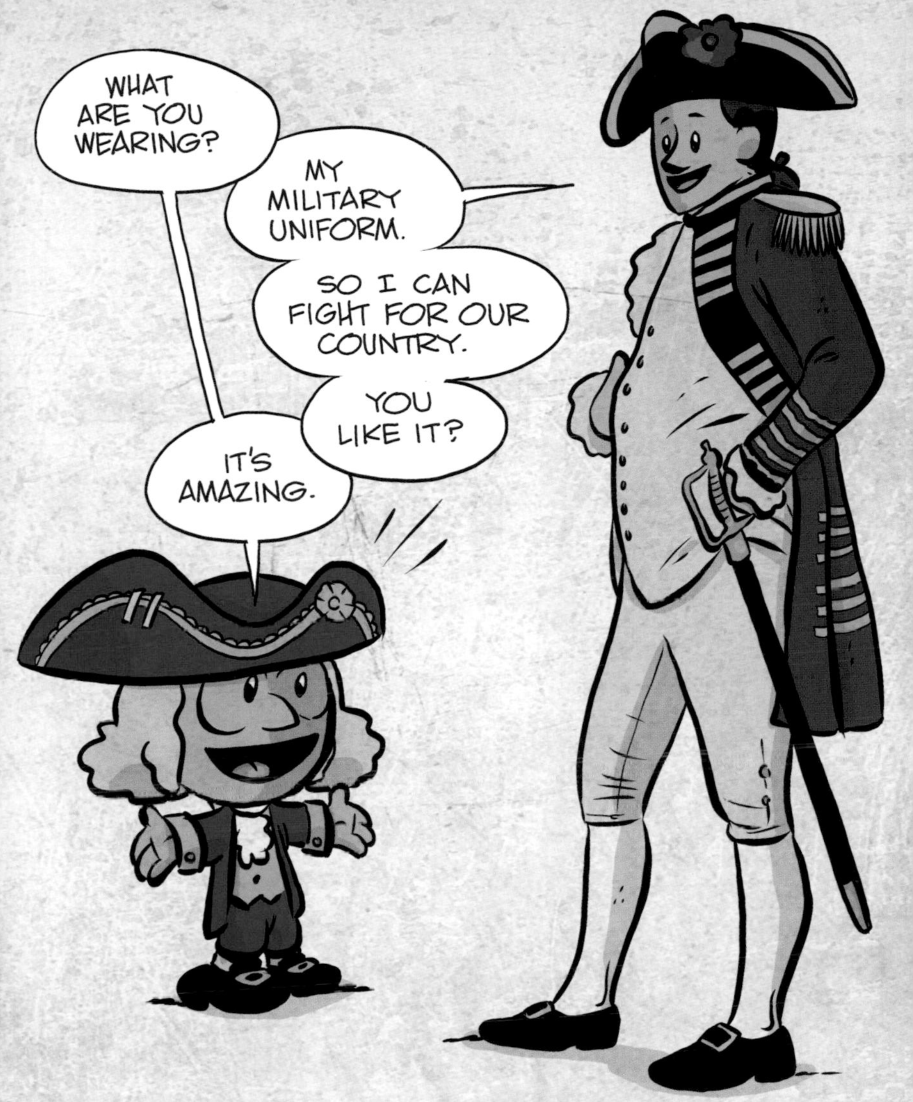
WHAT ARE YOU WEARING?
MY MILITARY UNIFORM.
SO I CAN FIGHT FOR OUR COUNTRY.
YOU LIKE IT?
IT'S AMAZING.

I loved hearing the stories of his adventures.

Thanks to my brother, I knew I wanted to serve in the military.

Soon, though, I saw how uncertain life could be.

When I was eleven, my dad died.

We couldn't afford proper schooling so my brothers had to teach me at home.

I didn't go to high school or college.

But I was committed to learning and building myself.

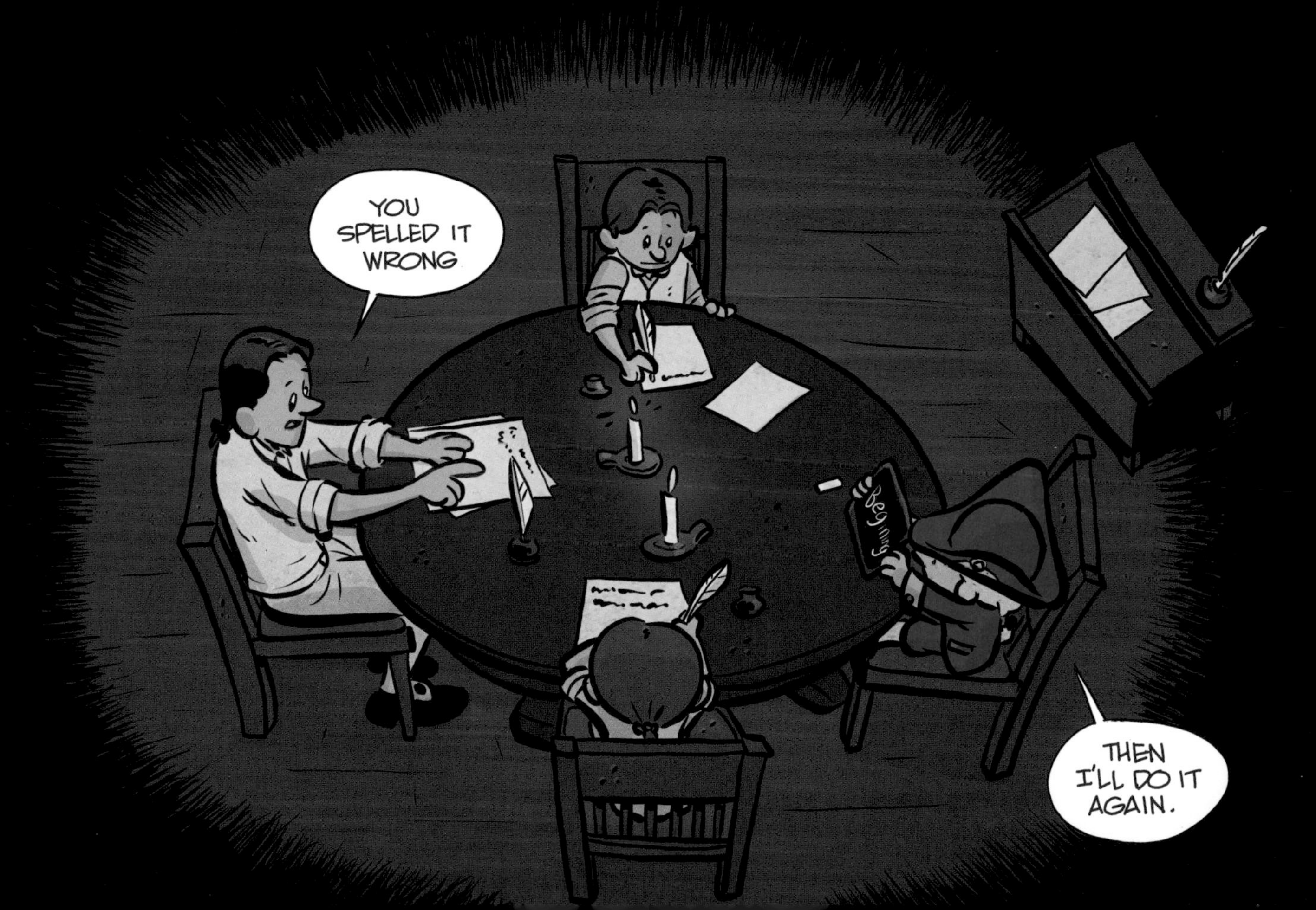
YOU SPELLED IT WRONG
THEN I'LL DO IT AGAIN.

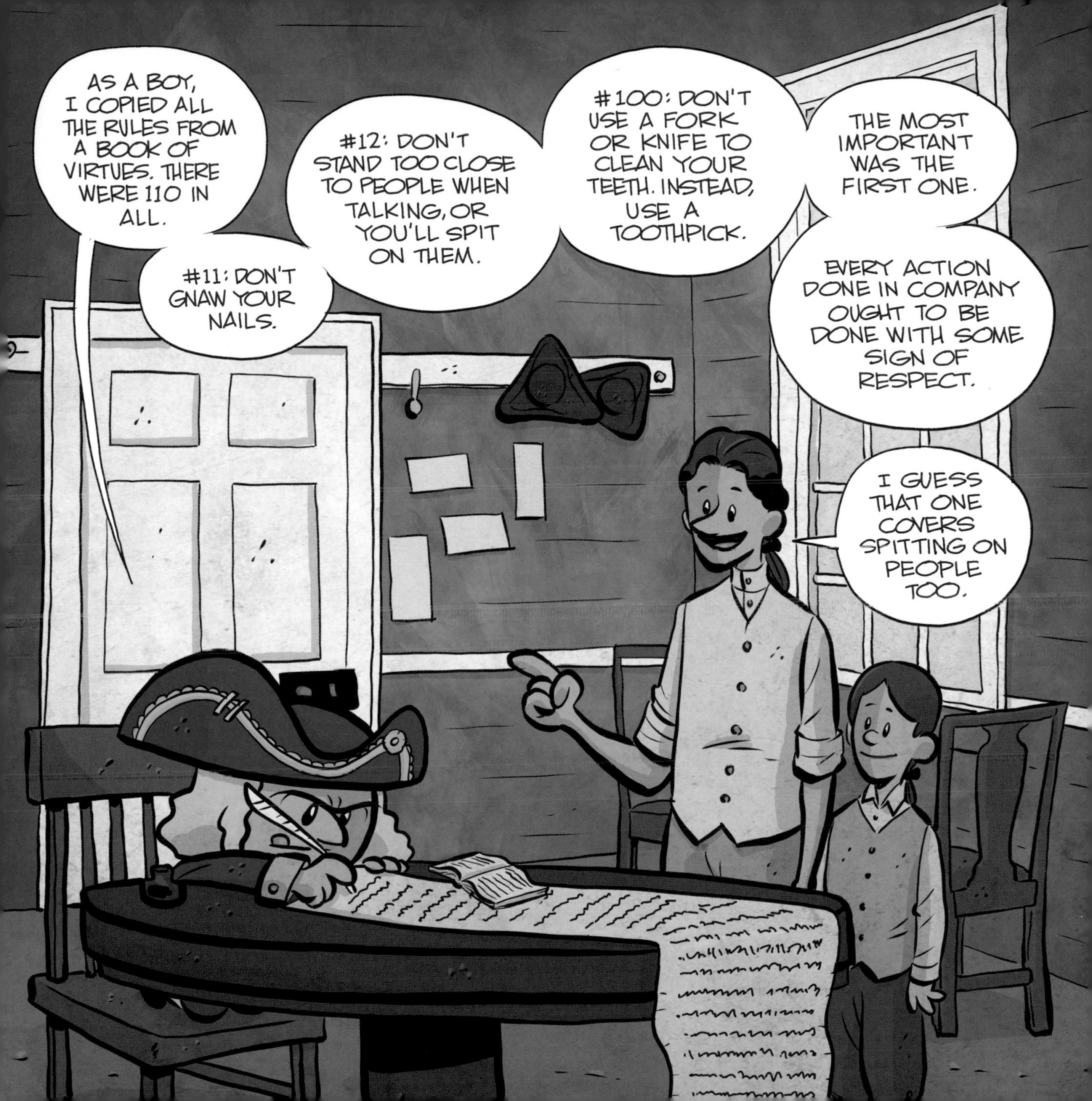
AS A BOY, I COPIED ALL THE RULES FROM A BOOK OF VIRTUES. THERE WERE 110 IN ALL.
#11: DON'T GNAW YOUR NAILS.
#12: DON'T STAND TOO CLOSE TO PEOPLE WHEN TALKING, OR YOU'LL SPIT ON THEM.
#100: DON'T USE A FORK OR KNIFE TO CLEAN YOUR TEETH. INSTEAD, USE A TOOTHPICK.
THE MOST IMPORTANT WAS THE FIRST ONE.
EVERY ACTION DONE IN COMPANY OUGHT TO BE DONE WITH SOME SIGN OF RESPECT.
I GUESS THAT ONE COVERS SPITTING ON PEOPLE TOO.

When I turned fifteen, my mother told me I needed to get a job.

Since I was good at math and precision, I became a surveyor, someone who explores large areas of land to find their boundaries.

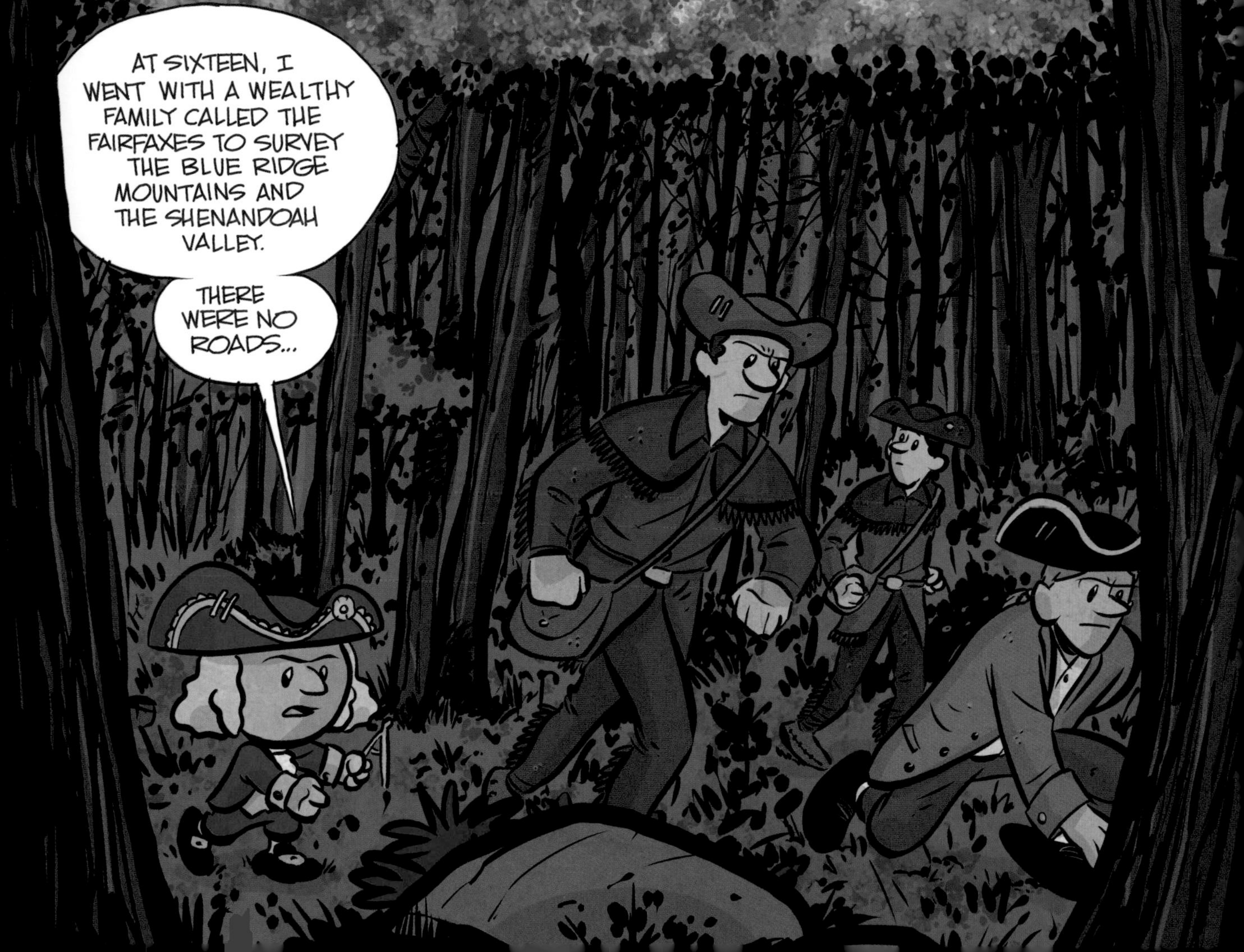
AT SIXTEEN, I WENT WITH A WEALTHY FAMILY CALLED THE FAIRFAXES TO SURVEY THE BLUE RIDGE MOUNTAINS AND THE SHENANDOAH VALLEY.
THERE WERE NO ROADS...

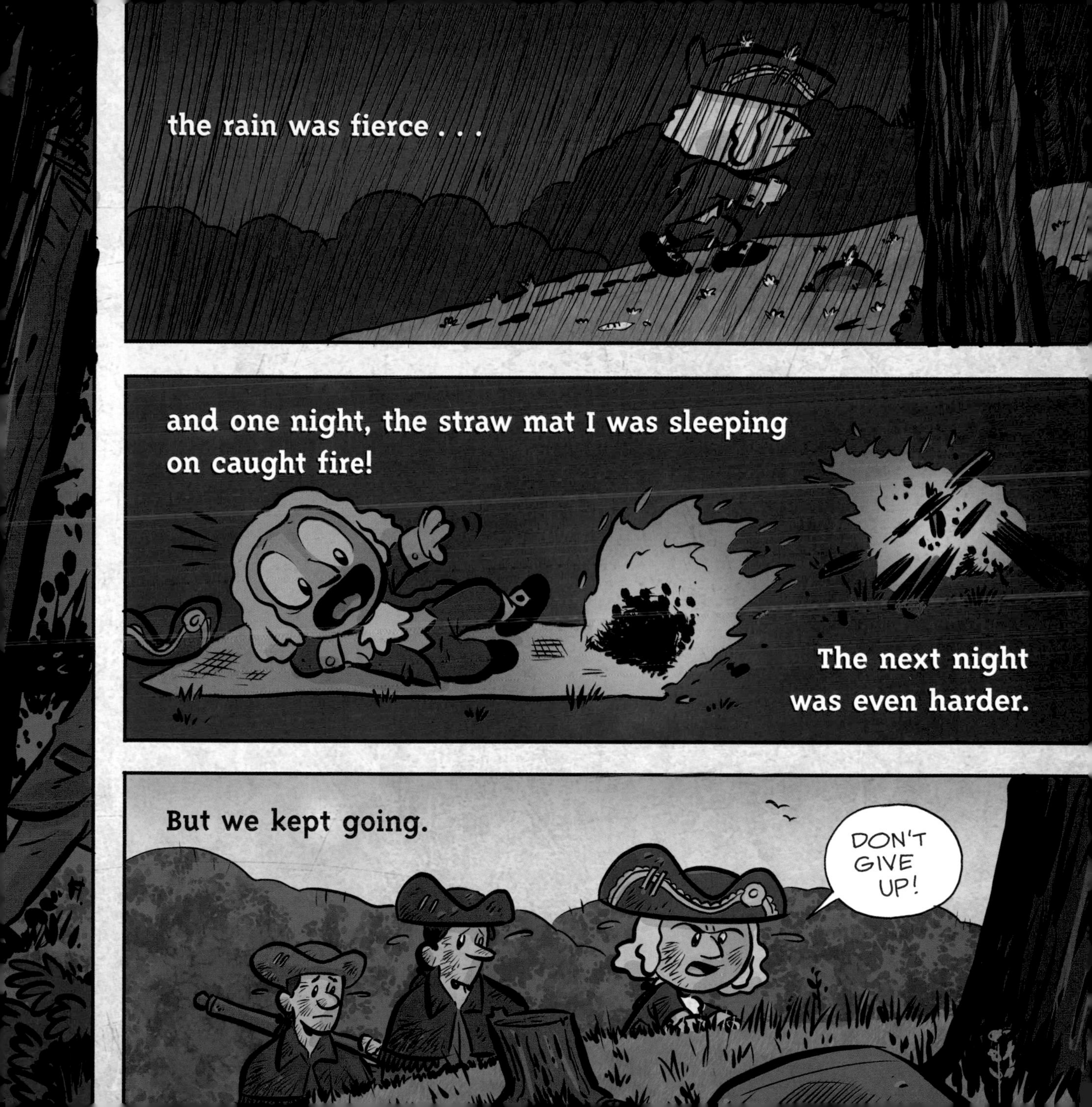
the rain was fierce . . .
and one night, the straw mat I was sleeping on caught fire!
The next night was even harder.
But we kept going.
DON'T GIVE UP!

There was something special in treading a new path, something beautiful in doing what no one had ever done before.

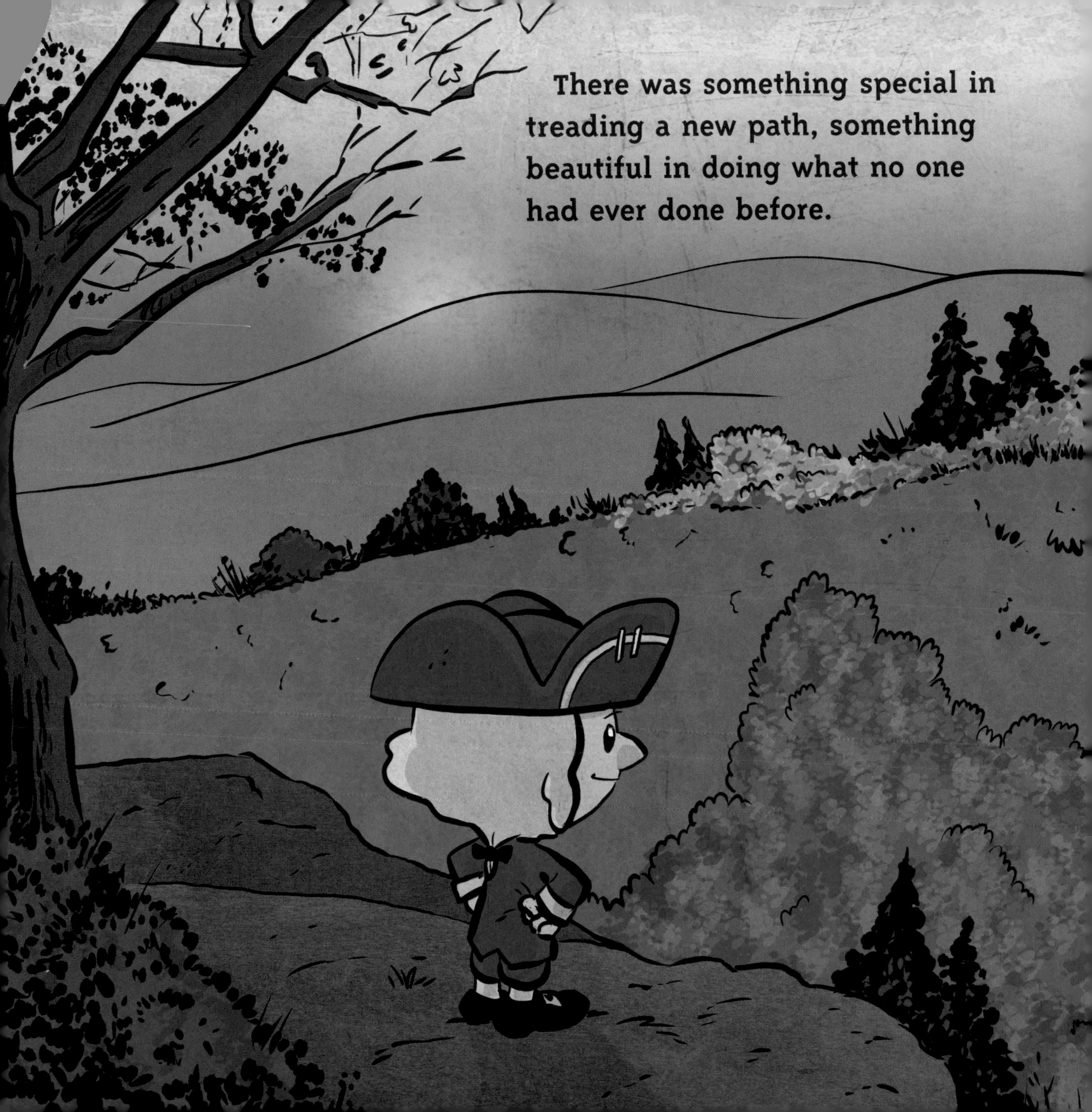

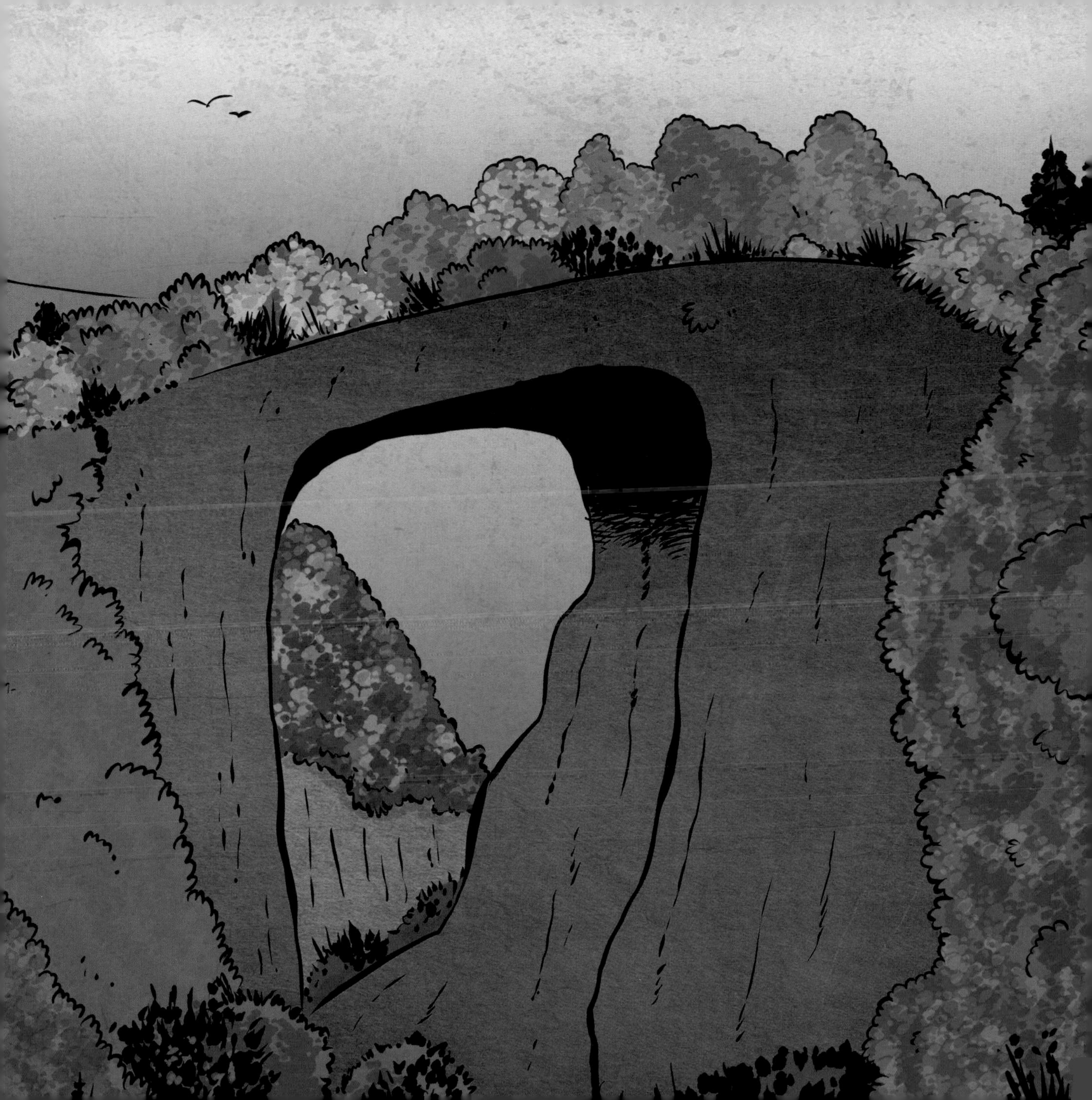

Just being around the Fairfaxes changed my life.
They helped me get work.
I observed how they lived, how they dressed, and how they ate.
I even learned how to properly . . .

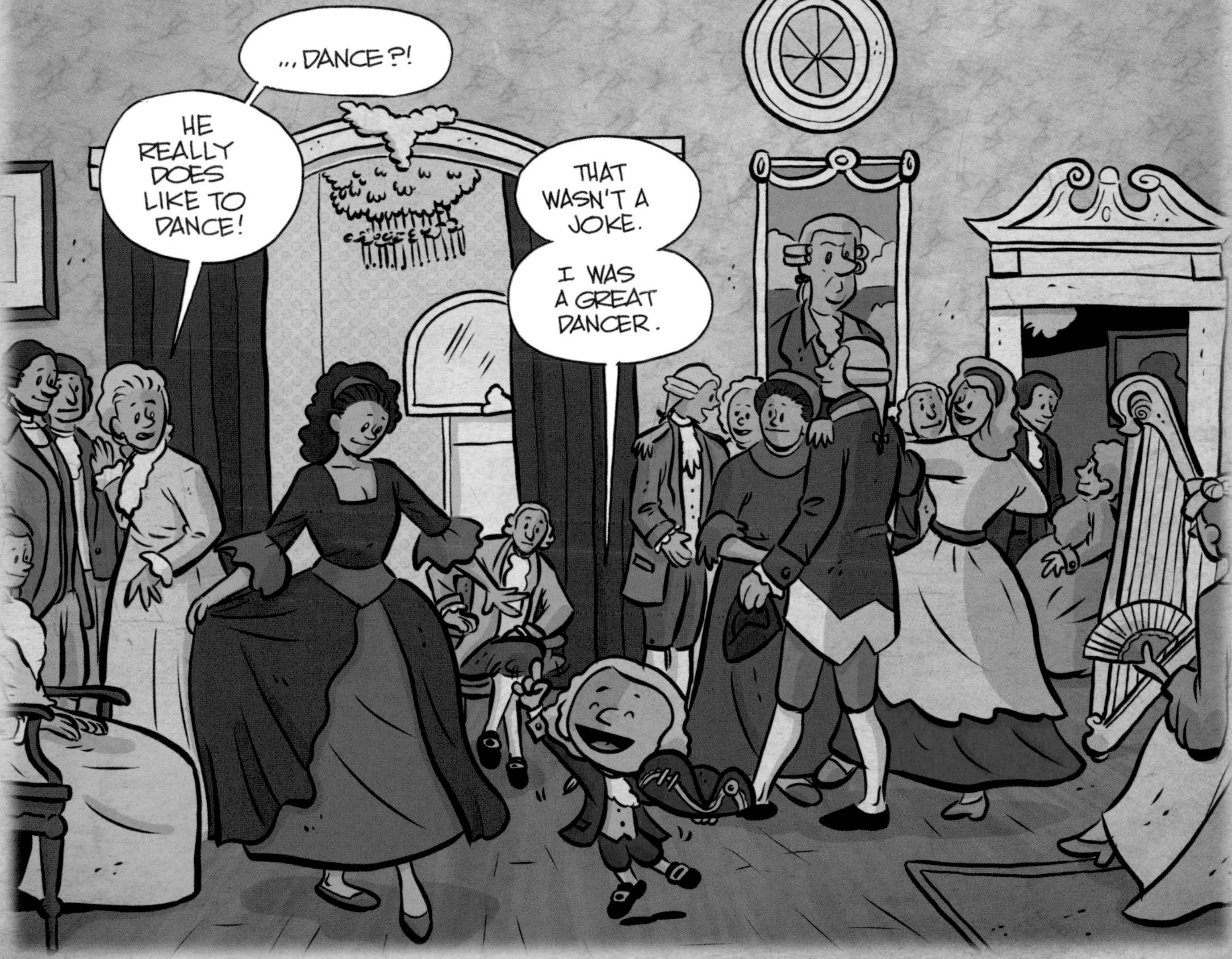
...DANCE?!
HE REALLY DOES LIKE TO DANCE!
THAT WASN'T A JOKE.
I WAS A GREAT DANCER.

At the Fairfaxes',
I ate with fine silver
and beautiful china.

At home, I ate with
sticks at a fire.
It was as if I was
living in two worlds.
But to me, both were
equally important.

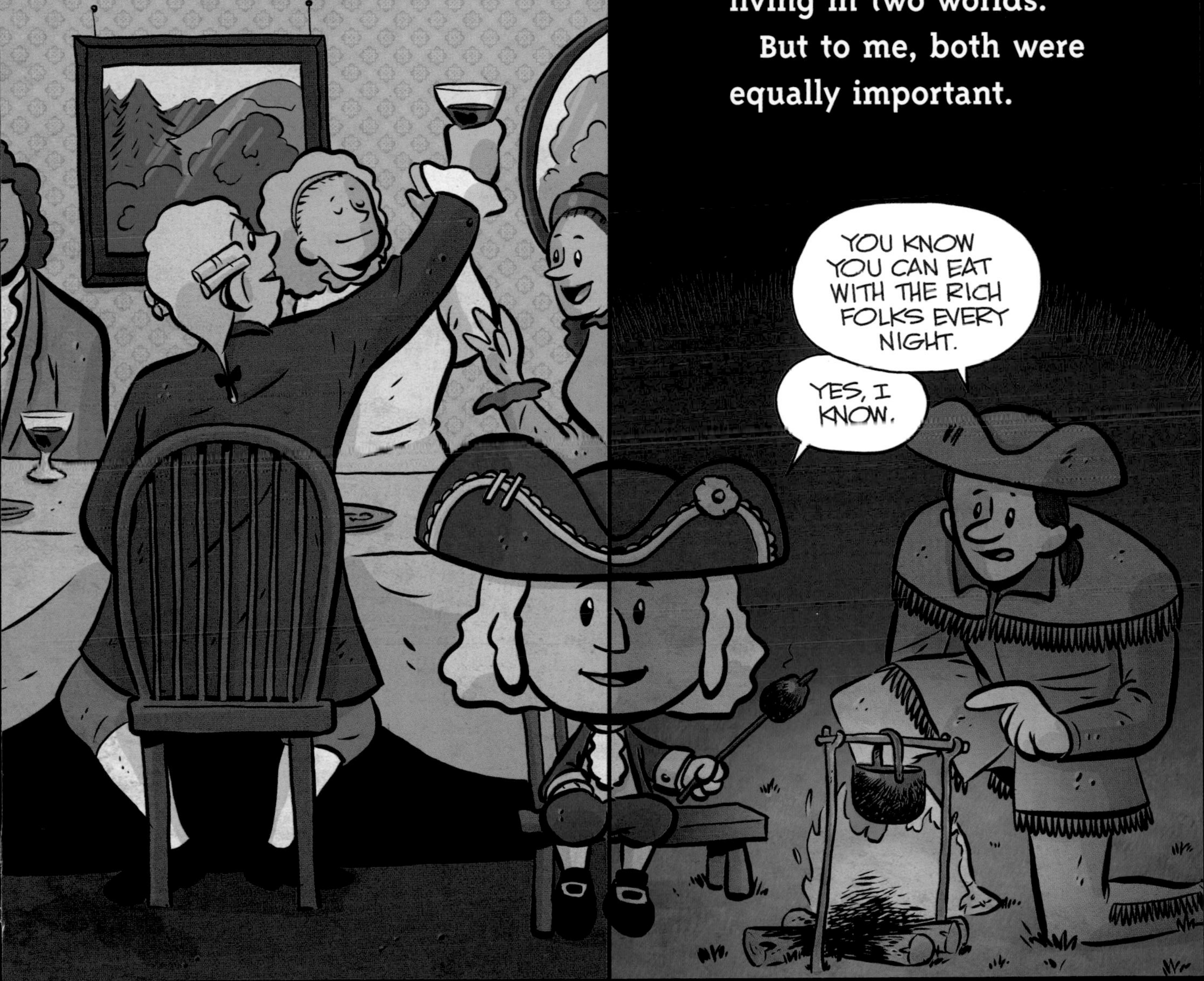

YOU KNOW YOU CAN EAT WITH THE RICH FOLKS EVERY NIGHT.
YES, I KNOW.

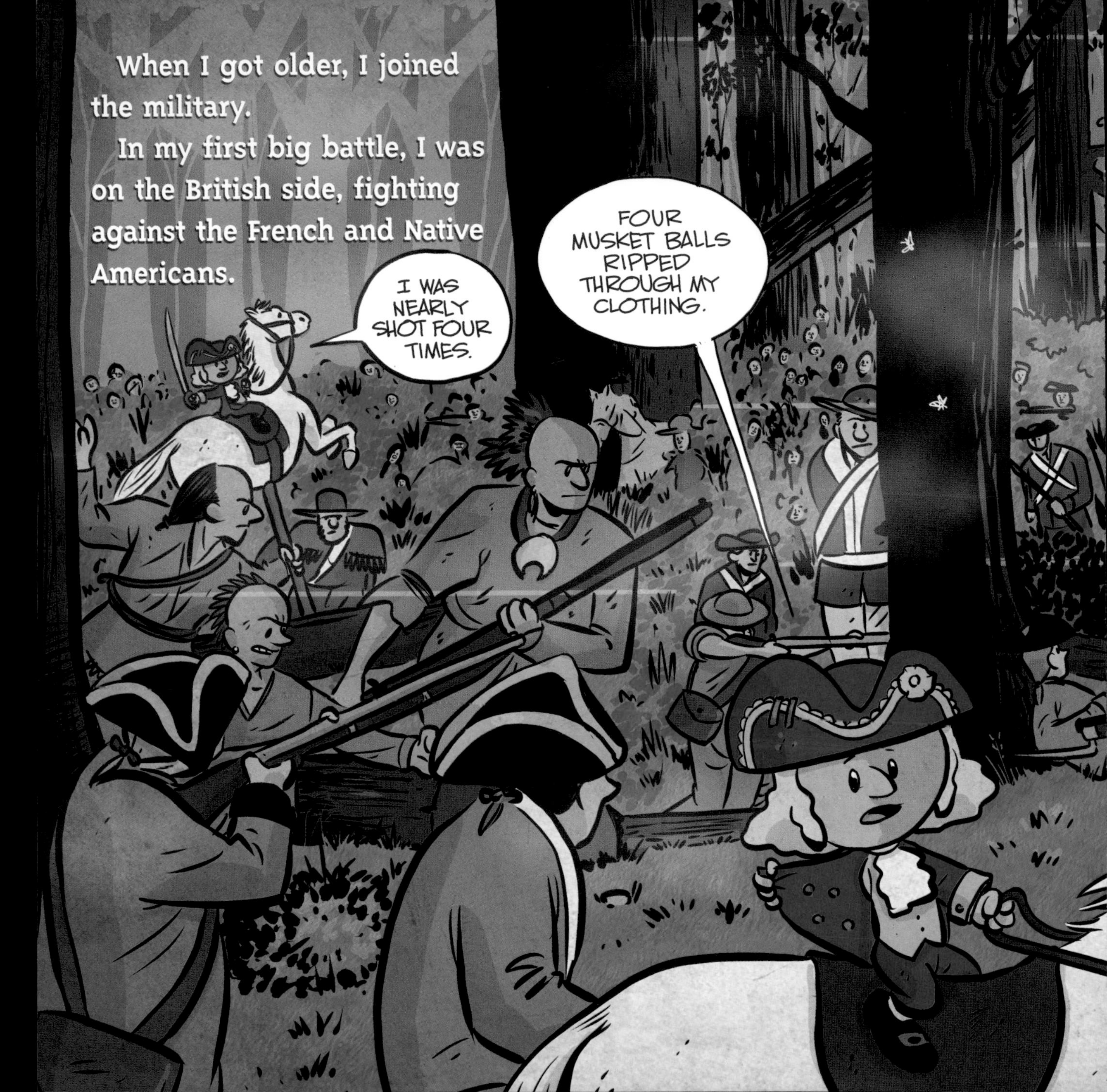
When I got older, I joined the military.
In my first big battle, I was on the British side, fighting against the French and Native Americans.
I WAS NEARLY SHOT FOUR TIMES.
FOUR MUSKET BALLS RIPPED THROUGH MY CLOTHING.

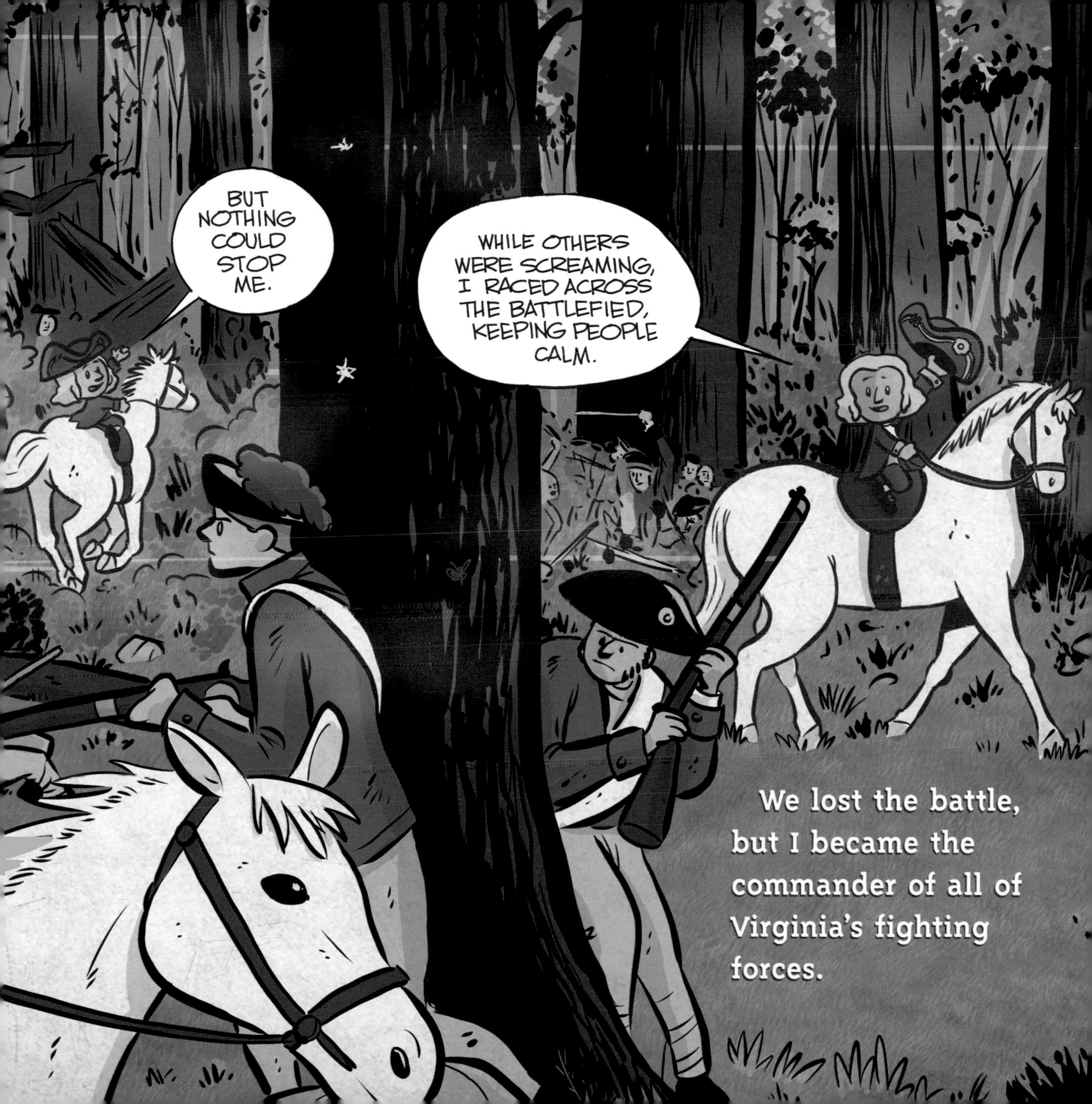
BUT NOTHING COULD STOP ME.
WHILE OTHERS WERE SCREAMING, I RACED ACROSS THE BATTLEFIED, KEEPING PEOPLE CALM.

We lost the battle, but I became the commander of all of Virginia's fighting forces.

At the age of twenty-three, I ran for office: to be a member of the house of the Virginia legislature.

I lost.

That's right. I lost.

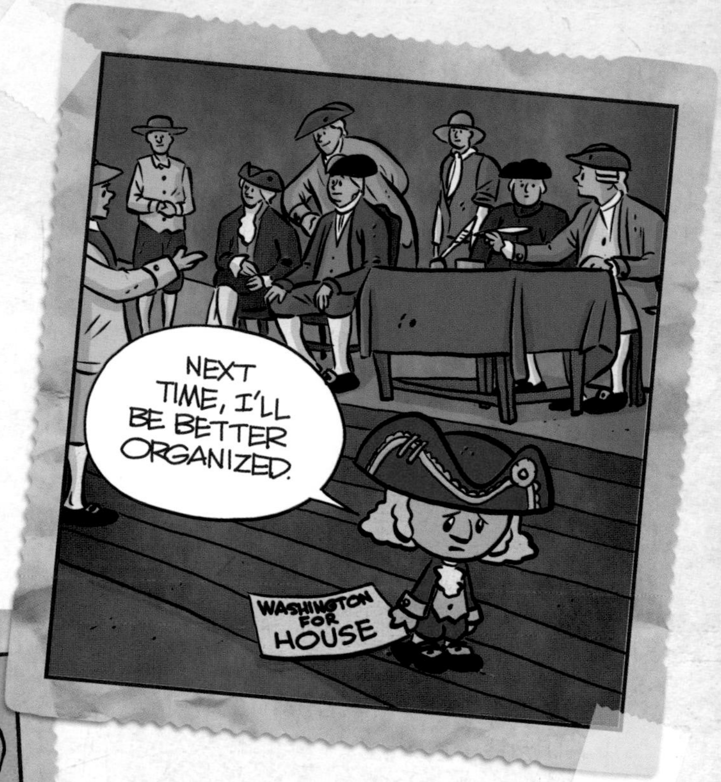
NEXT TIME, I'LL BE BETTER ORGANIZED.
WASHINGTON FOR HOUSE

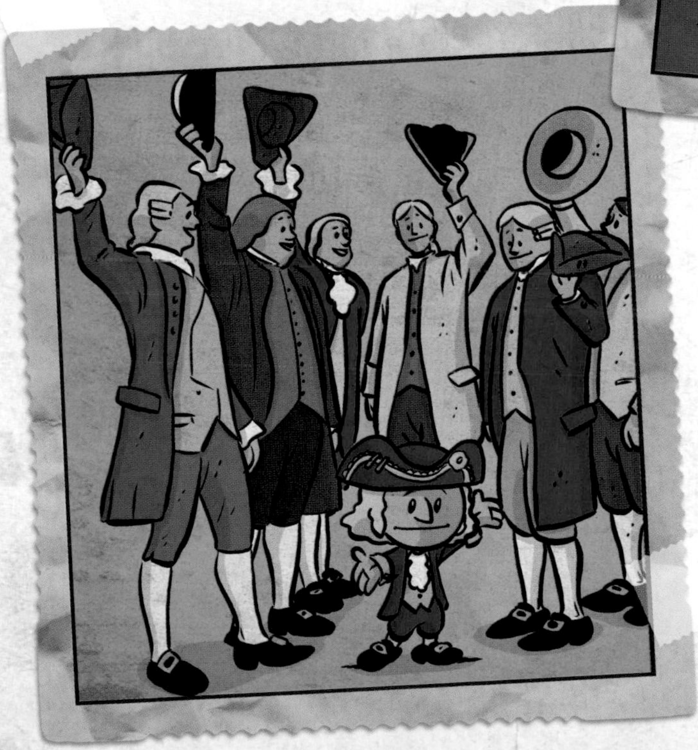

It didn't stop me. I tried again, and this time, I won.

In fact, I won reelection every time after that. But the world as I knew it . . .

was about to change.

Remember, when I was growing up, the United States didn't exist yet.

Back then, there were no states—just colonies, all of them controlled by England.

We were ruled by the British king, named George III.

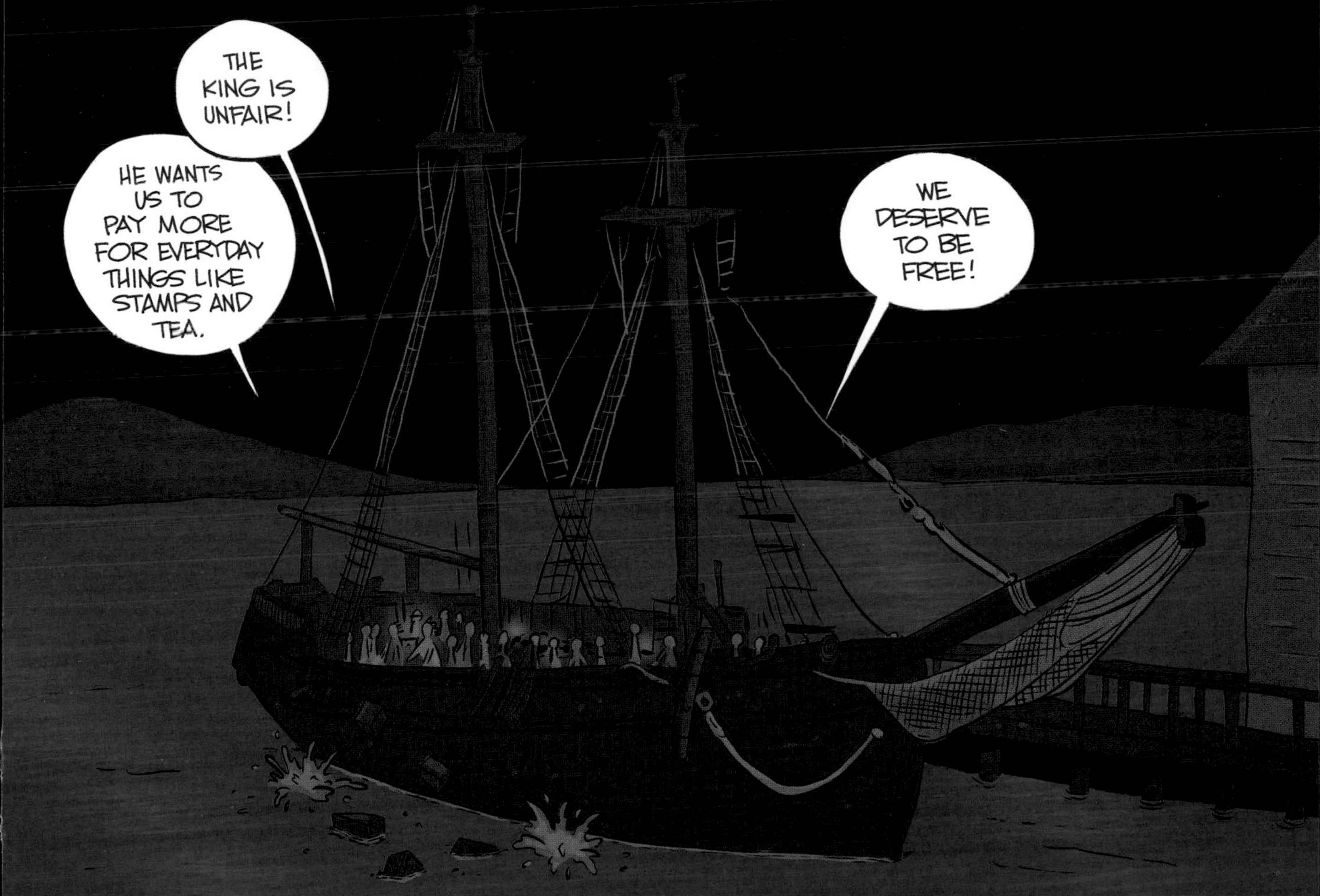
THE KING IS UNFAIR!
HE WANTS US TO PAY MORE FOR EVERYDAY THINGS LIKE STAMPS AND TEA.
WE DESERVE TO BE FREE!

In April 1775, the first shots were fired in Massachusetts, in Lexington and Concord.

It took eight days for the news of this new "American Revolution" to reach me.

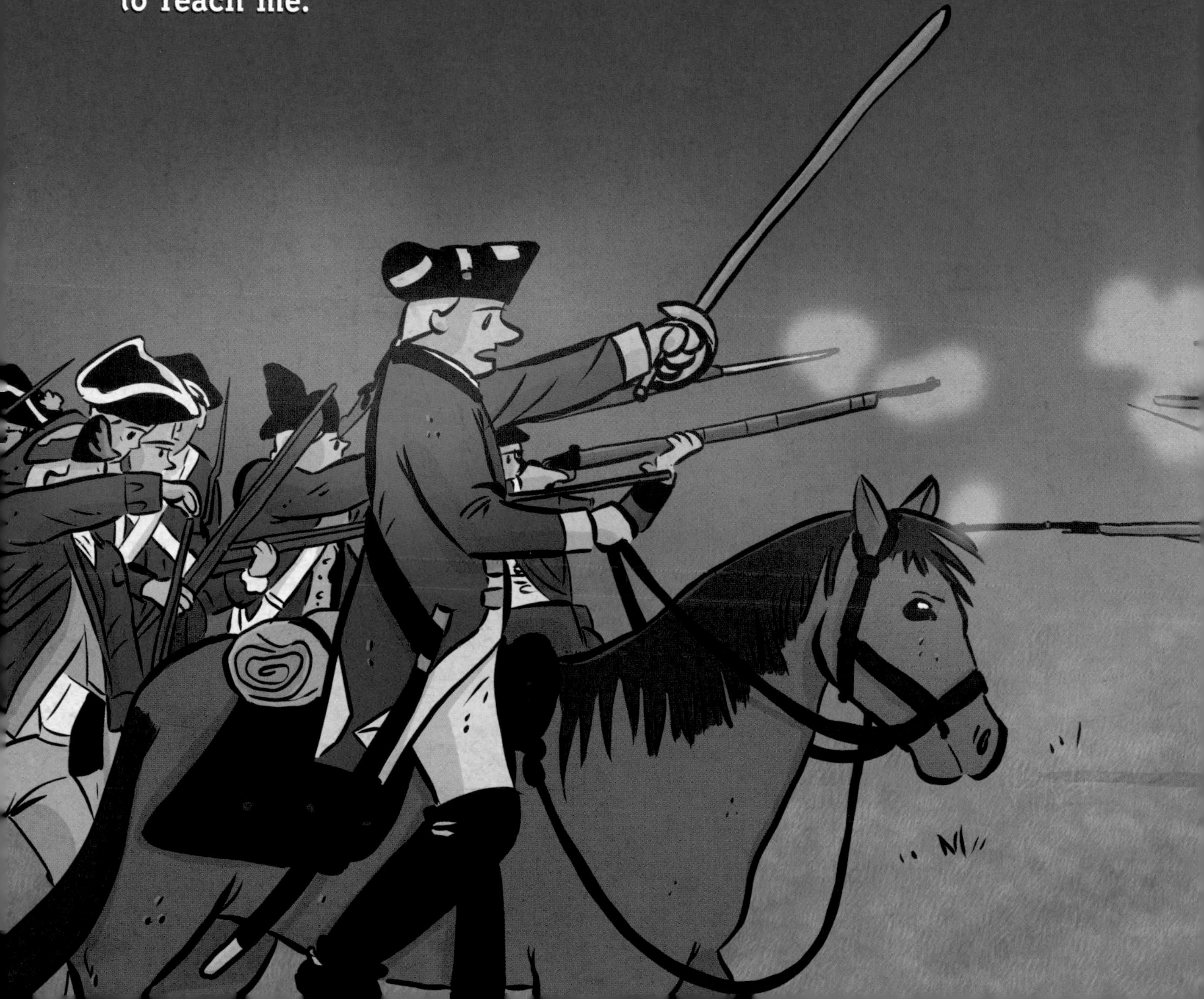

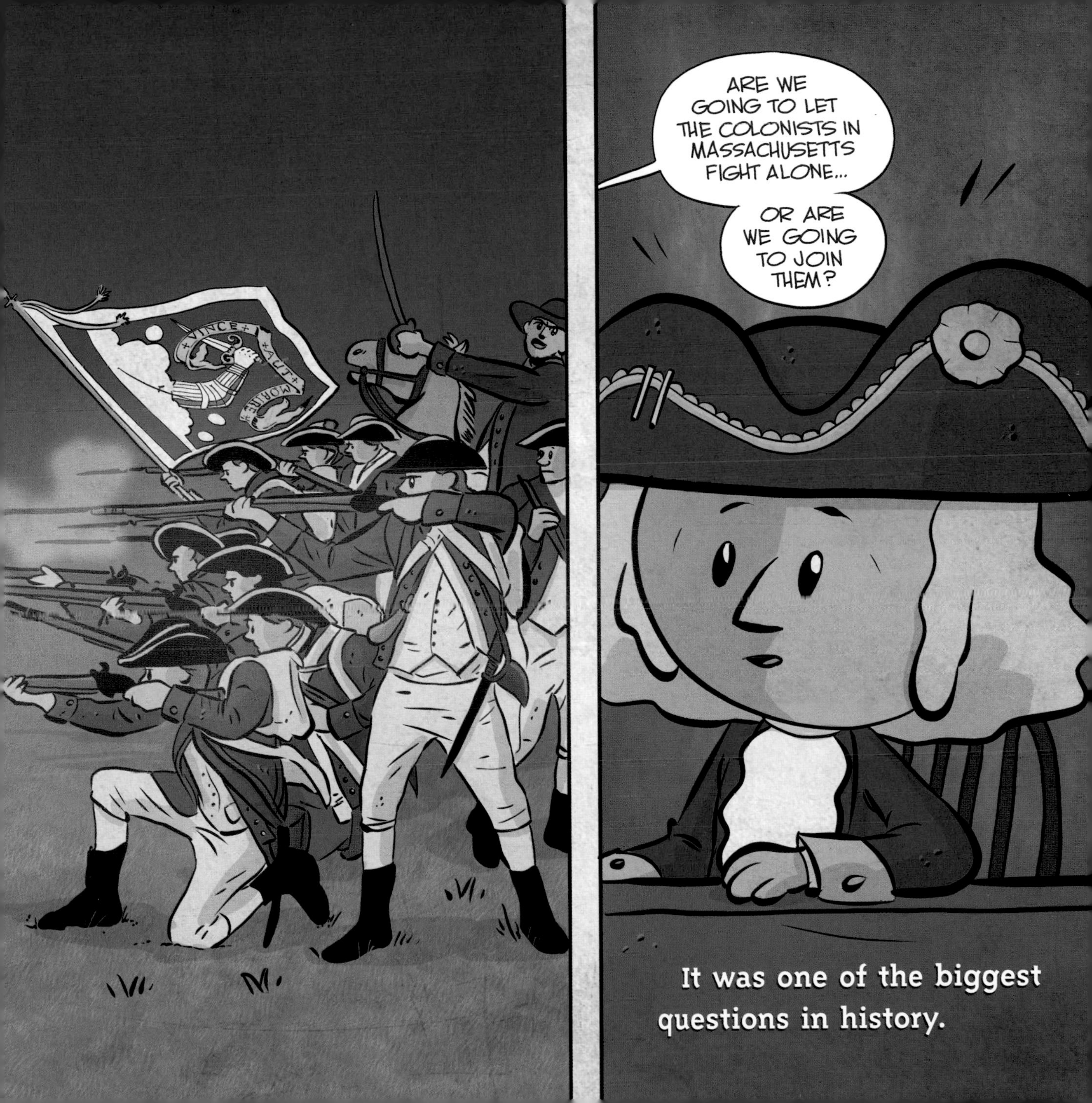
VINCE AUT MORIRE
ARE WE GOING TO LET THE COLONISTS IN MASSACHUSETTS FIGHT ALONE...
OR ARE WE GOING TO JOIN THEM?
It was one of the biggest questions in history.

The answer came at a meeting called the Second Continental Congress.

Our thirteen colonies decided we would fight together against King George III.

All we needed was a leader for the battle.

Guess who they chose?

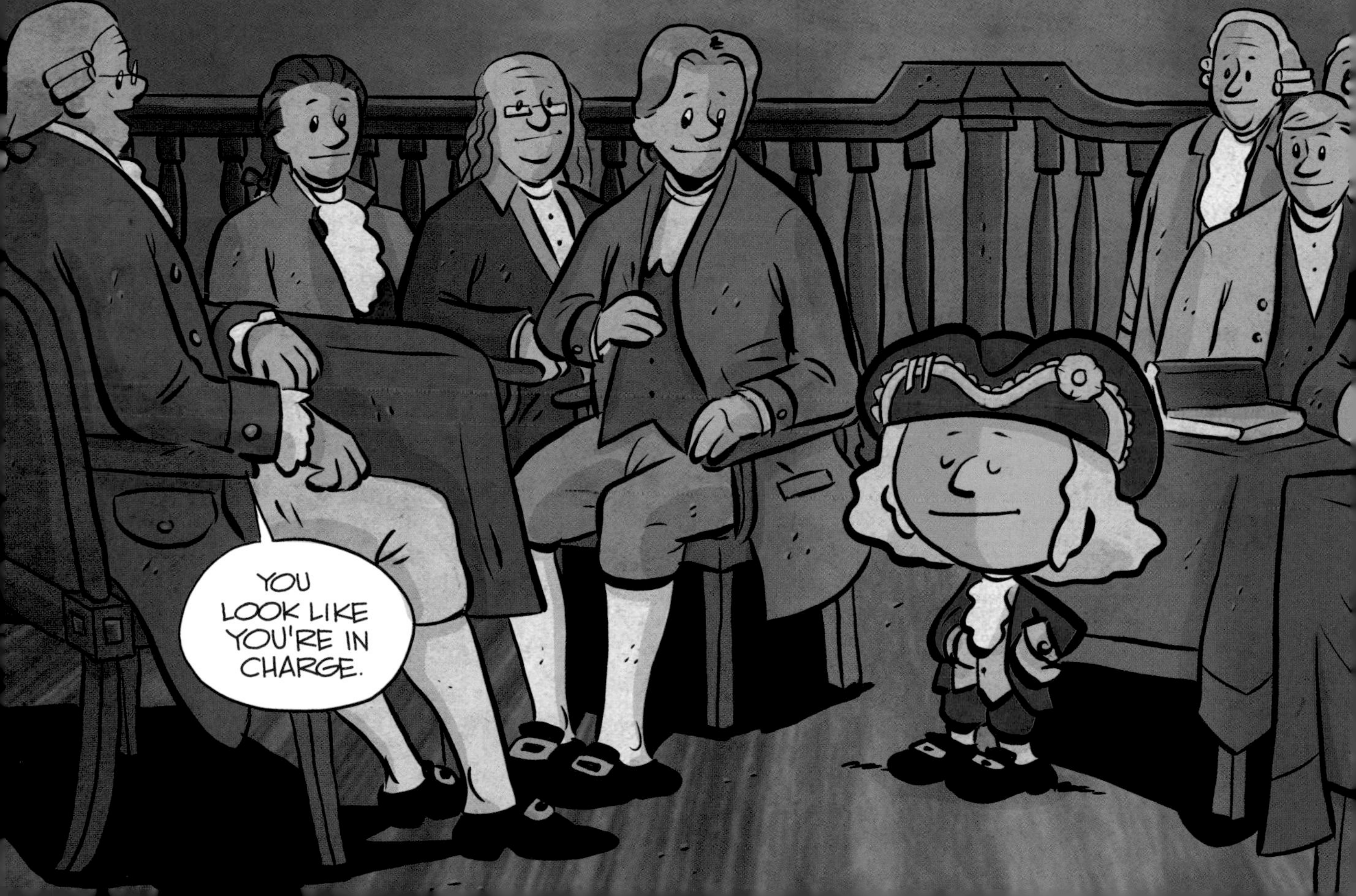
YOU LOOK LIKE YOU'RE IN CHARGE.

Some say it was because I was a natural leader.
Some say it was simply because I was taller than everyone else.
But let me tell you a secret: I was the only one wearing a military uniform.

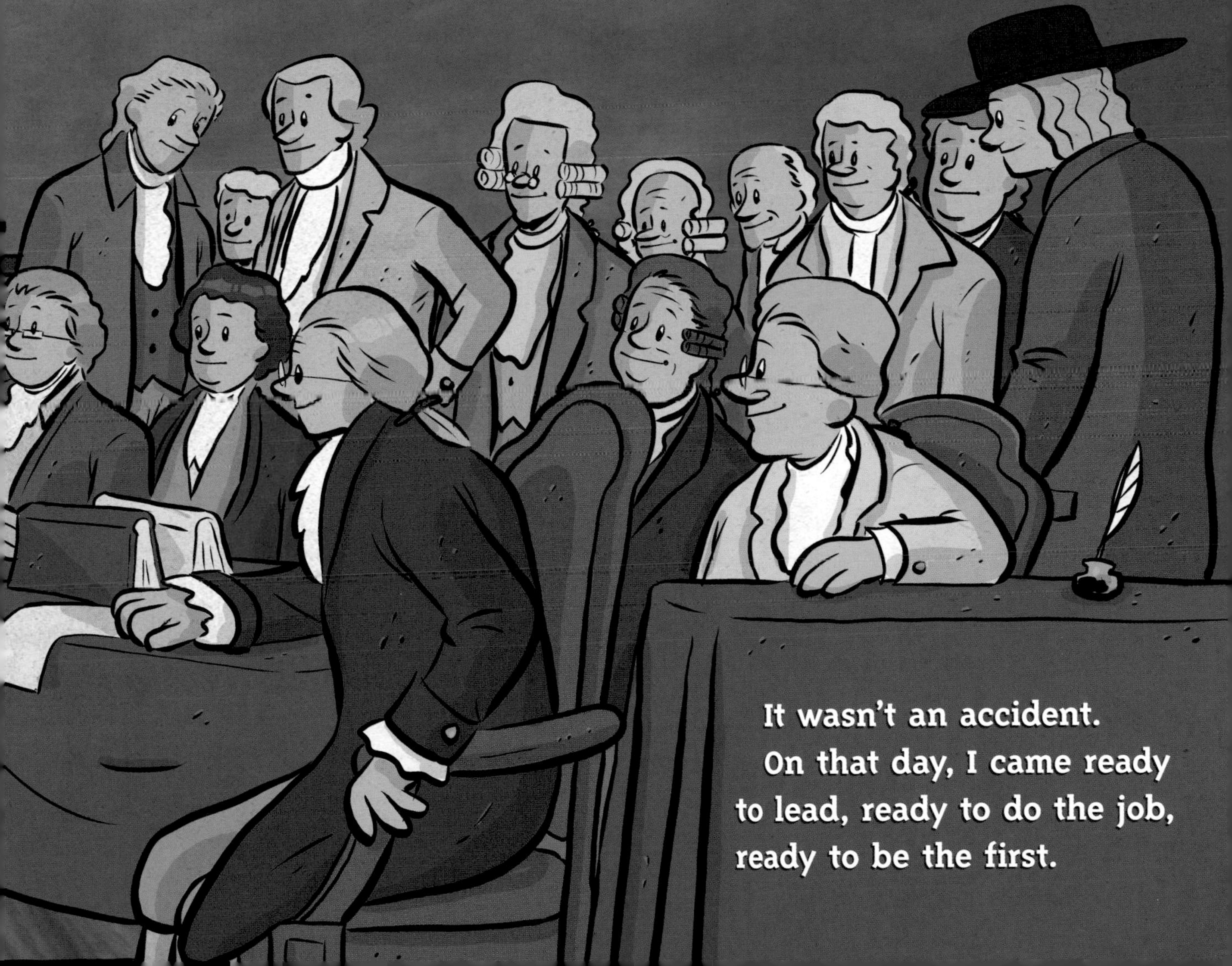

It wasn't an accident.
On that day, I came ready to lead, ready to do the job, ready to be the first.

Was it easy to be in power?

Never.

Our side didn't have enough food, clothing, or weapons.

Their side was well fed and well armed.

Our side didn't have trained soldiers. We were farmers and fishermen.

Their side was the greatest fighting force in the world.

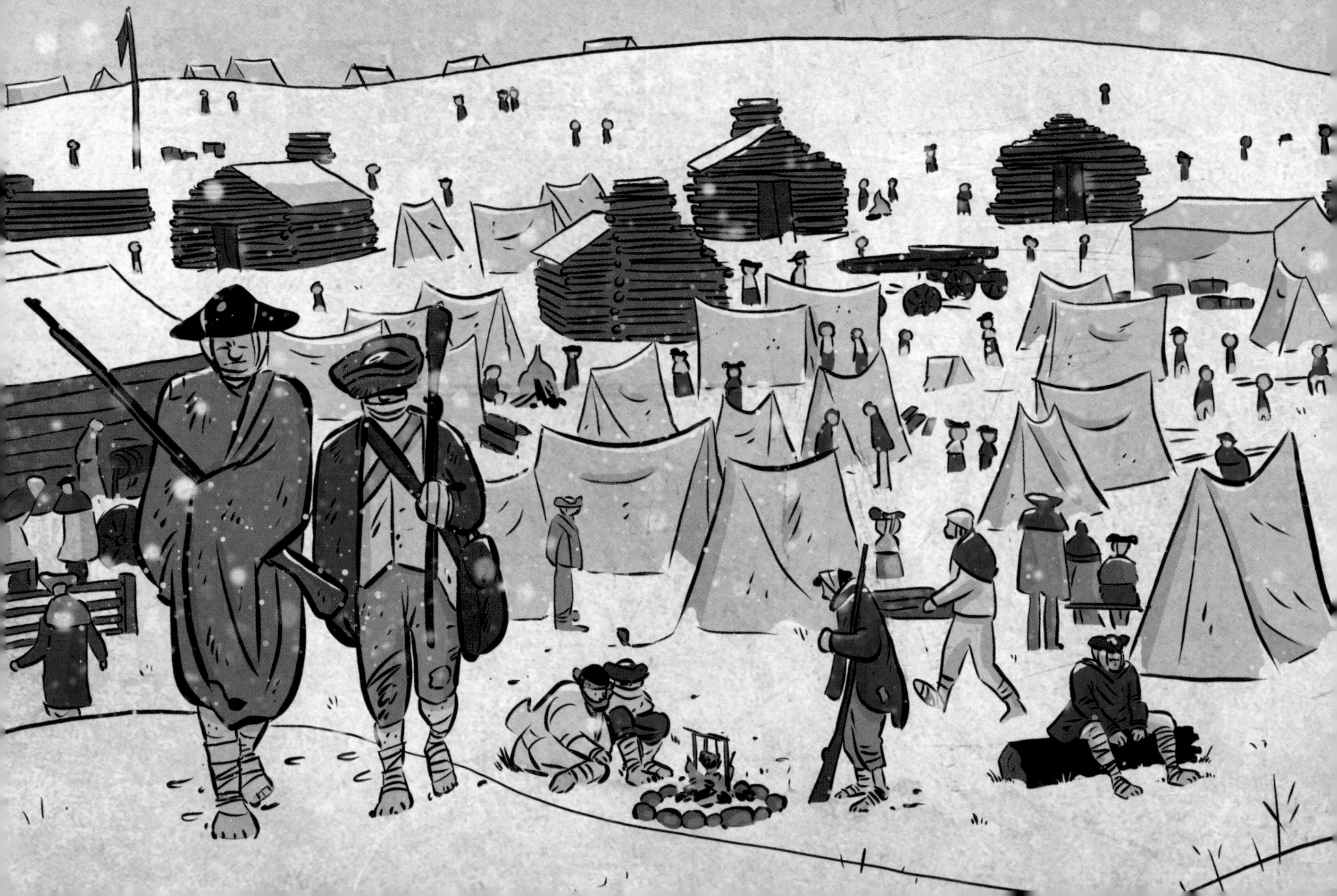

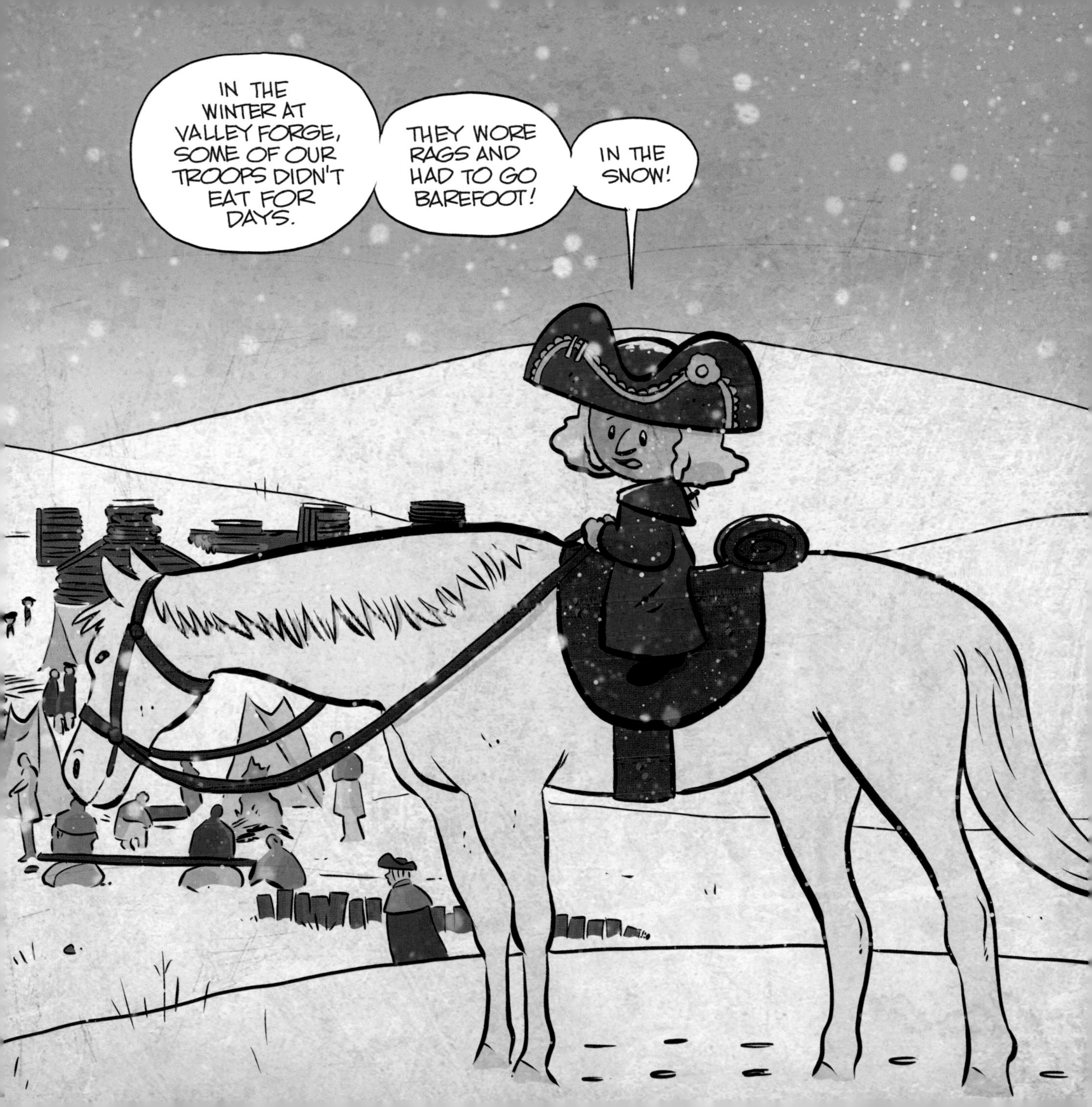
IN THE WINTER AT VALLEY FORGE, SOME OF OUR TROOPS DIDN'T EAT FOR DAYS.
THEY WORE RAGS AND HAD TO GO BAREFOOT!
IN THE SNOW!

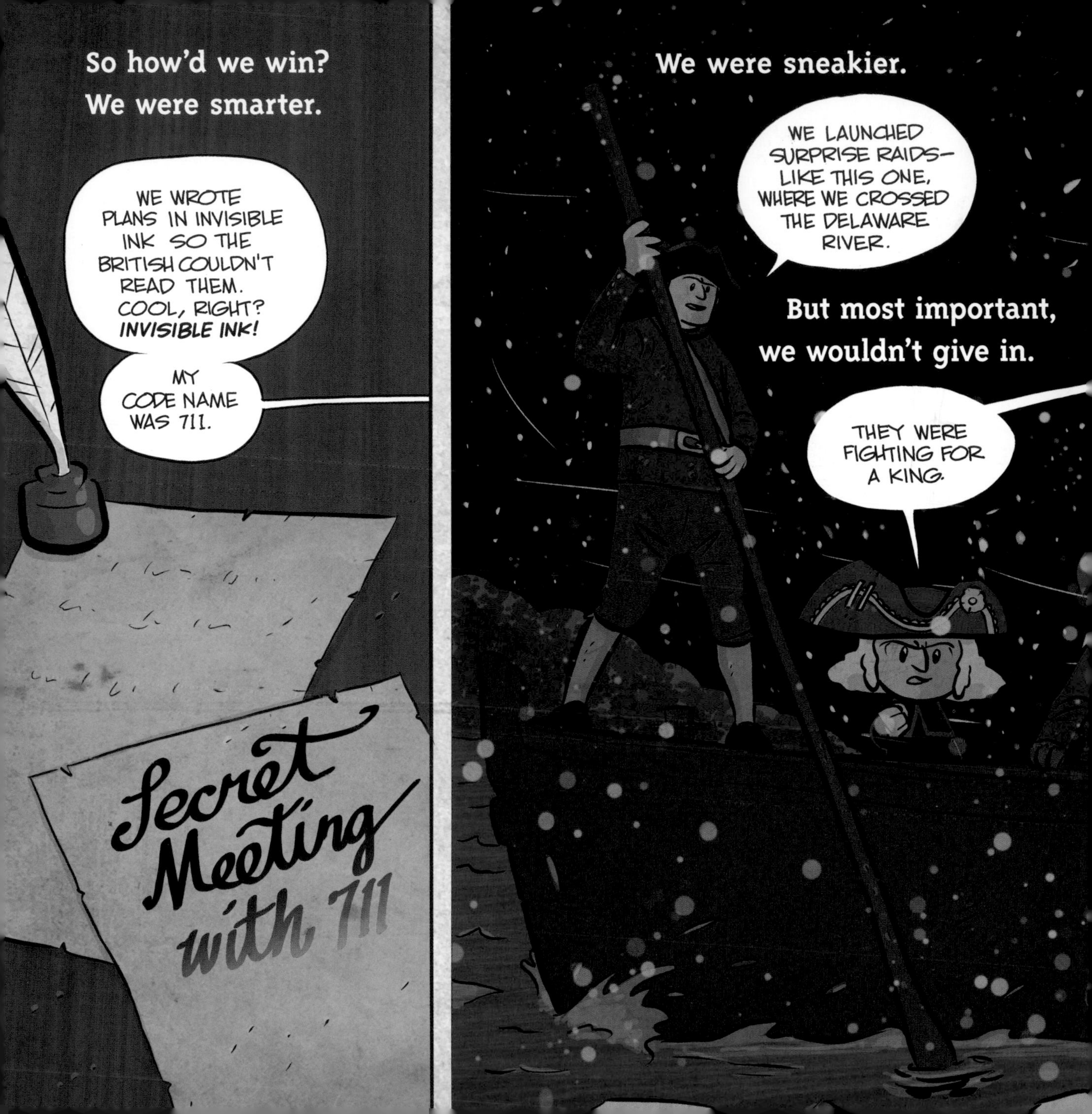
So how'd we win?
We were smarter.
WE WROTE PLANS IN INVISIBLE INK SO THE BRITISH COULDN'T READ THEM. COOL, RIGHT? INVISIBLE INK!
MY CODE NAME WAS 711.
Secret Meeting with 711
We were sneakier.
WE LAUNCHED SURPRISE RAIDS— LIKE THIS ONE, WHERE WE CROSSED THE DELAWARE RIVER.
But most important, we wouldn't give in.
THEY WERE FIGHTING FOR A KING.

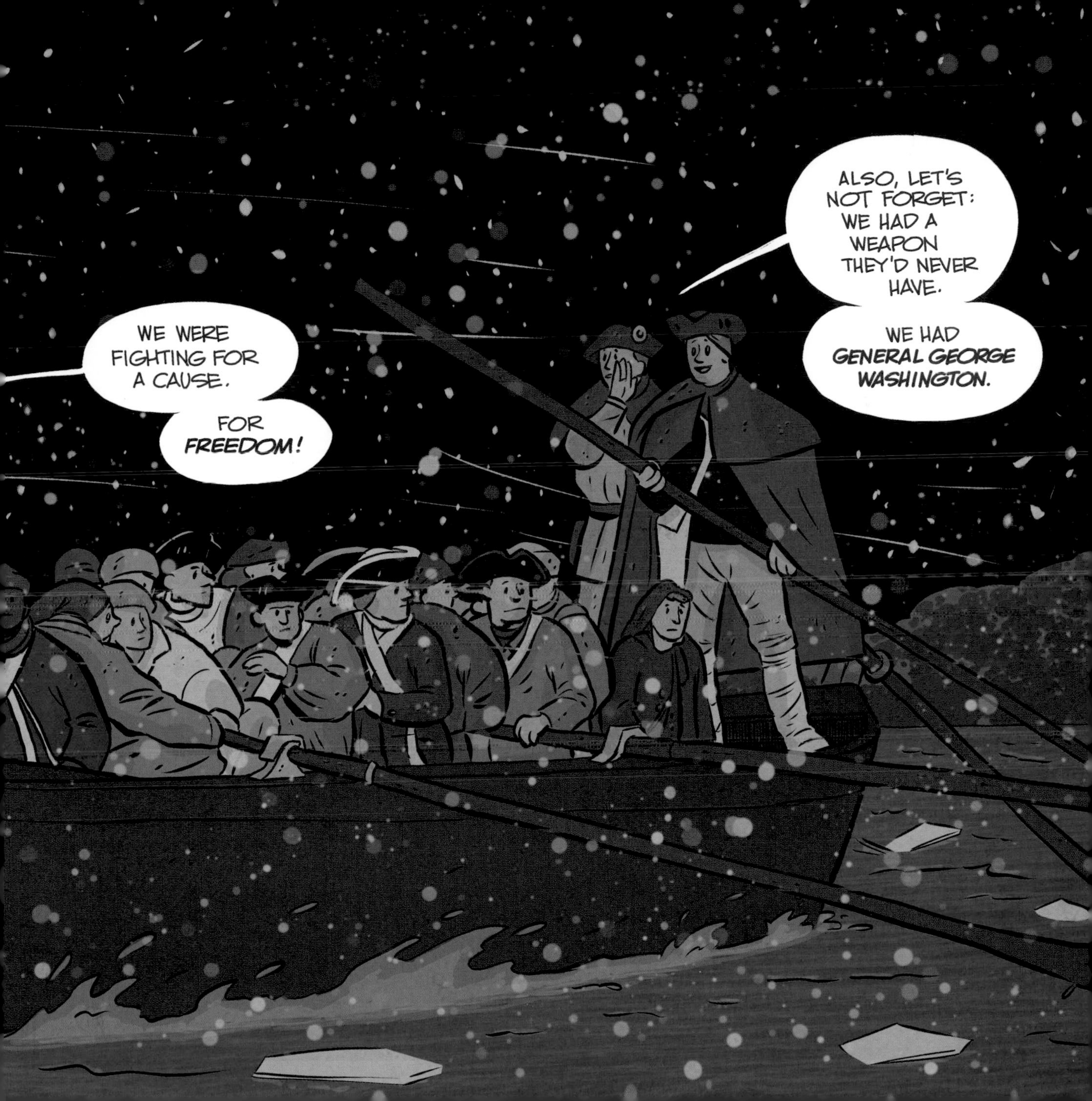
WE WERE FIGHTING FOR A CAUSE.
FOR FREEDOM!
ALSO, LET'S NOT FORGET: WE HAD A WEAPON THEY'D NEVER HAVE.
WE HAD GENERAL GEORGE WASHINGTON.

After we beat the British army, a new government was formed.

I presided over the convention that wrote our Constitution, which created the new laws for our country.

The brand-new United States of America was free to explore its own future.

Now all we needed was to pick our first president.

Someone brave.

Someone strong.

Someone trustworthy enough to handle all that power.

Again, guess who they chose?

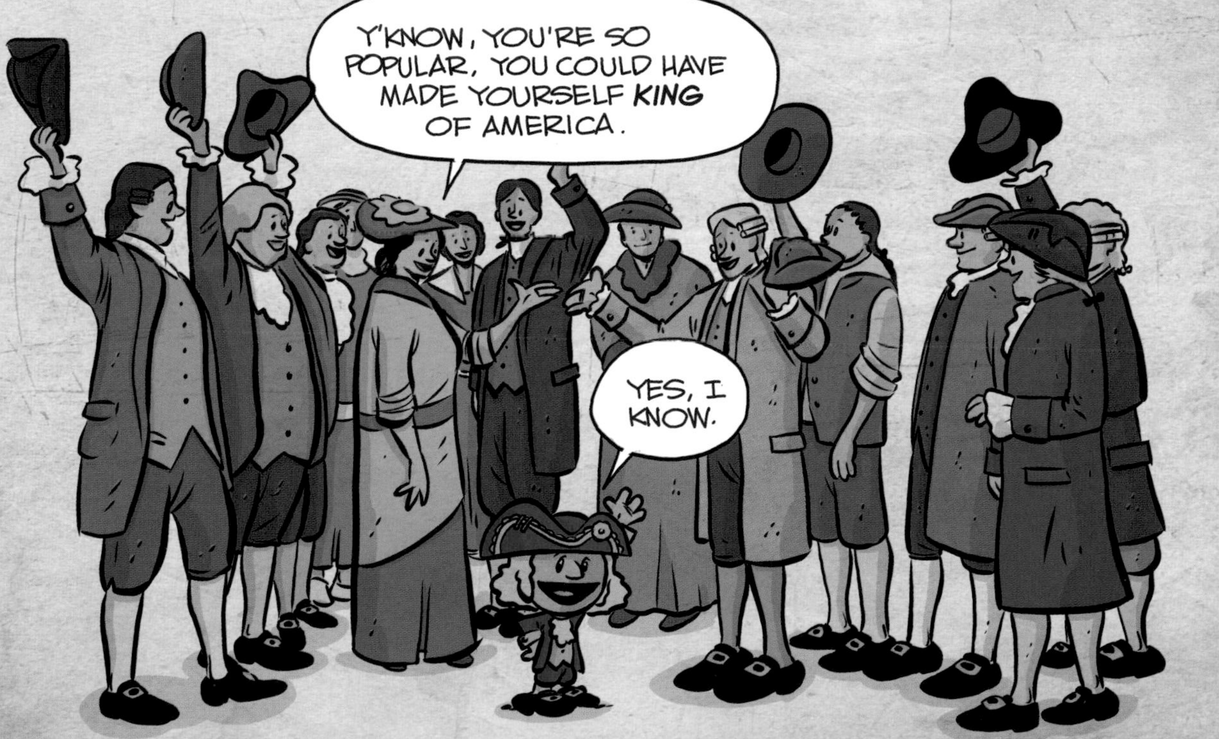
Y'KNOW, YOU'RE SO POPULAR, YOU COULD HAVE MADE YOURSELF **KING** OF AMERICA.
YES, I KNOW.

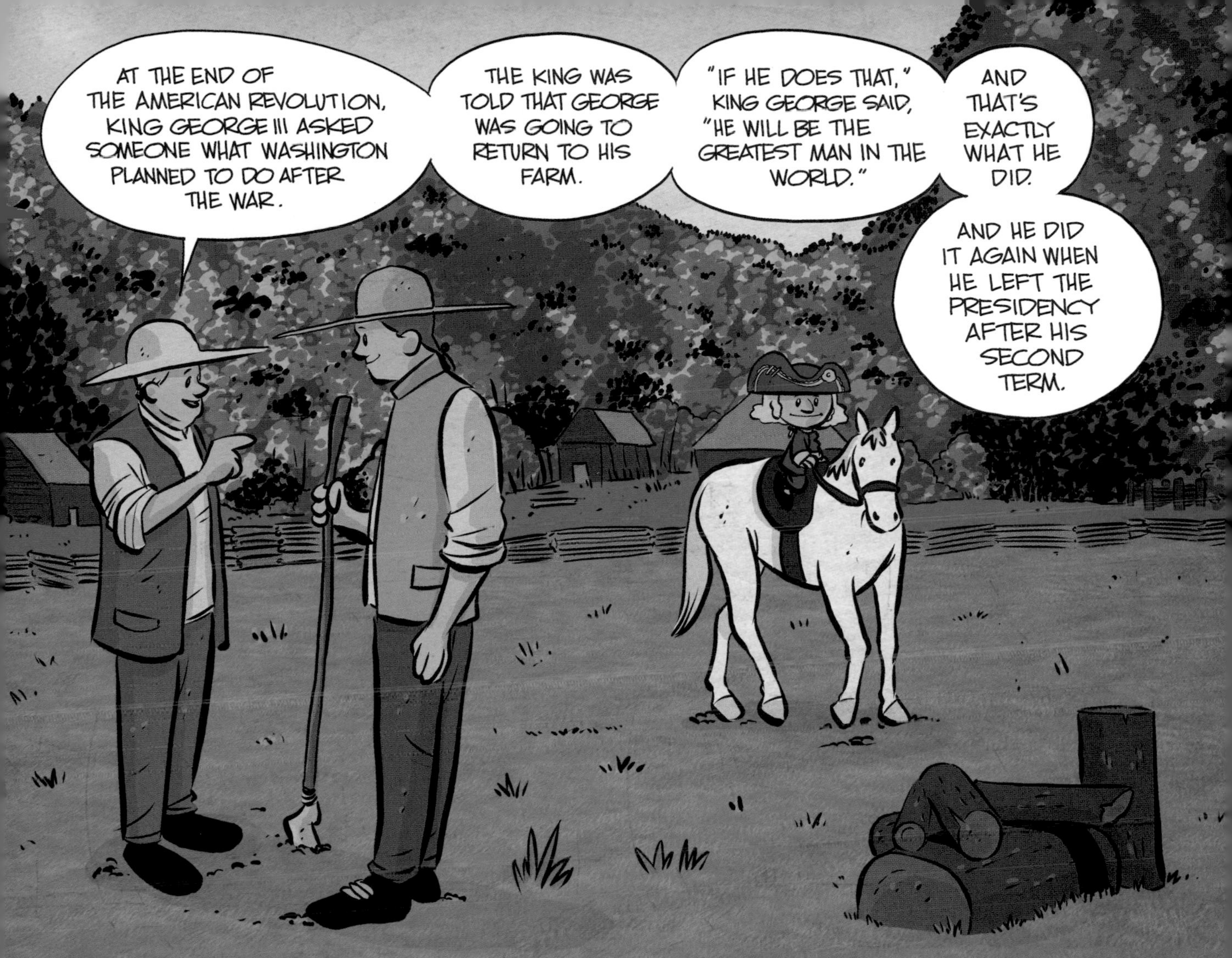
AT THE END OF THE AMERICAN REVOLUTION, KING GEORGE III ASKED SOMEONE WHAT WASHINGTON PLANNED TO DO AFTER THE WAR.
THE KING WAS TOLD THAT GEORGE WAS GOING TO RETURN TO HIS FARM.
"IF HE DOES THAT," KING GEORGE SAID, "HE WILL BE THE GREATEST MAN IN THE WORLD."
AND THAT'S EXACTLY WHAT HE DID.
AND HE DID IT AGAIN WHEN HE LEFT THE PRESIDENCY AFTER HIS SECOND TERM.

Some say it was my most heroic act.
Instead of putting myself first, I put my faith in my country.
I put my faith in you.

In life, there are many ways to lead.
You can be a quiet leader, a tough leader, a bold leader.
But leadership isn't about being in charge.
It's about taking care of those *in* your charge.

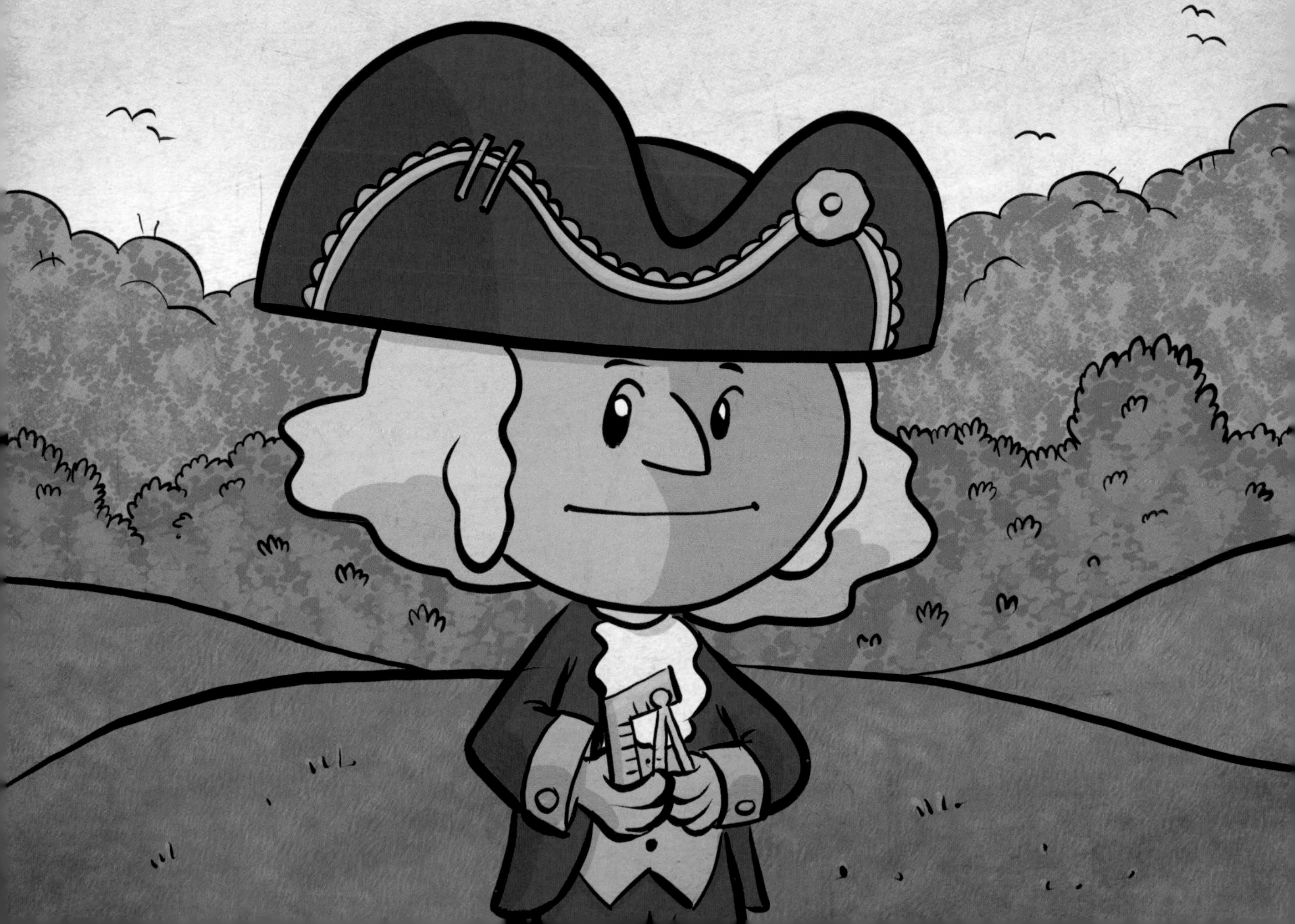

When you're in a position of power, always look out for those who put their faith in you.

And always forge your own road, because sometimes the most important trail is the one no one has ever taken before.

When you do those things, you will clear a path . . .

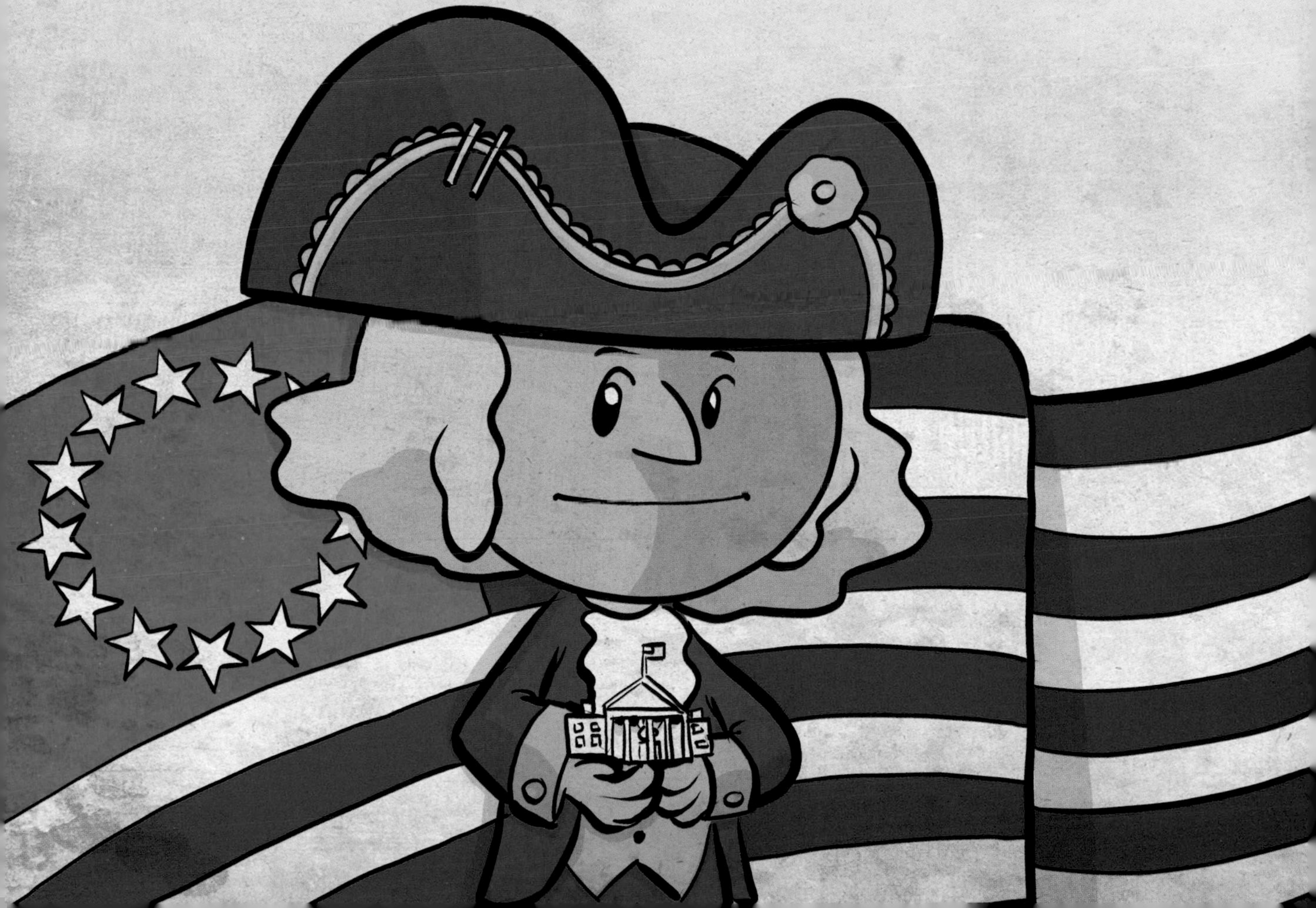

that will lead the way for others.

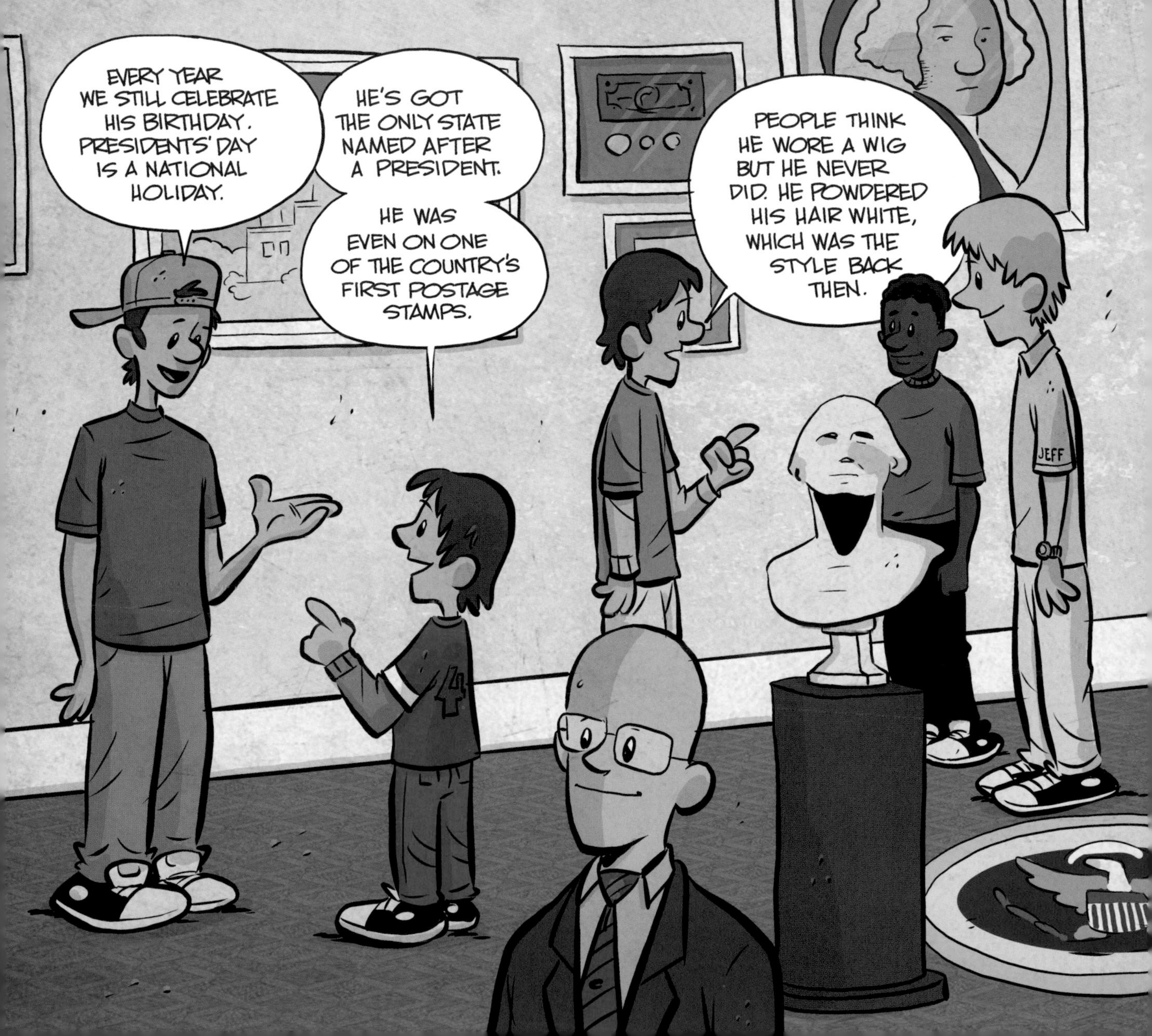
EVERY YEAR WE STILL CELEBRATE HIS BIRTHDAY. PRESIDENTS' DAY IS A NATIONAL HOLIDAY.
HE'S GOT THE ONLY STATE NAMED AFTER A PRESIDENT.
HE WAS EVEN ON ONE OF THE COUNTRY'S FIRST POSTAGE STAMPS.
PEOPLE THINK HE WORE A WIG BUT HE NEVER DID. HE POWDERED HIS HAIR WHITE, WHICH WAS THE STYLE BACK THEN.
JEFF

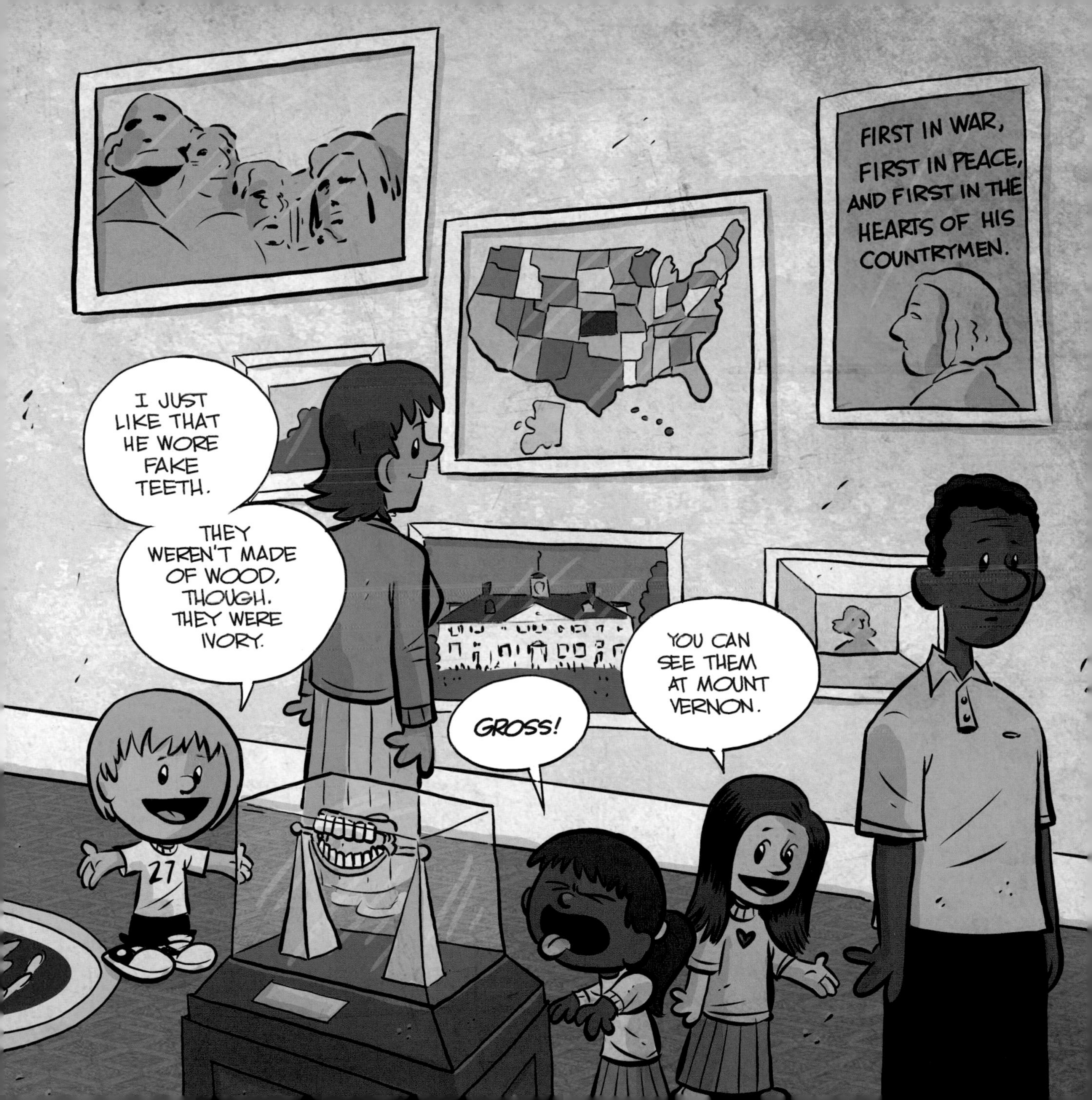
FIRST IN WAR, FIRST IN PEACE, AND FIRST IN THE HEARTS OF HIS COUNTRYMEN.
I JUST LIKE THAT HE WORE FAKE TEETH.
THEY WEREN'T MADE OF WOOD, THOUGH. THEY WERE IVORY.
GROSS!
YOU CAN SEE THEM AT MOUNT VERNON.
27

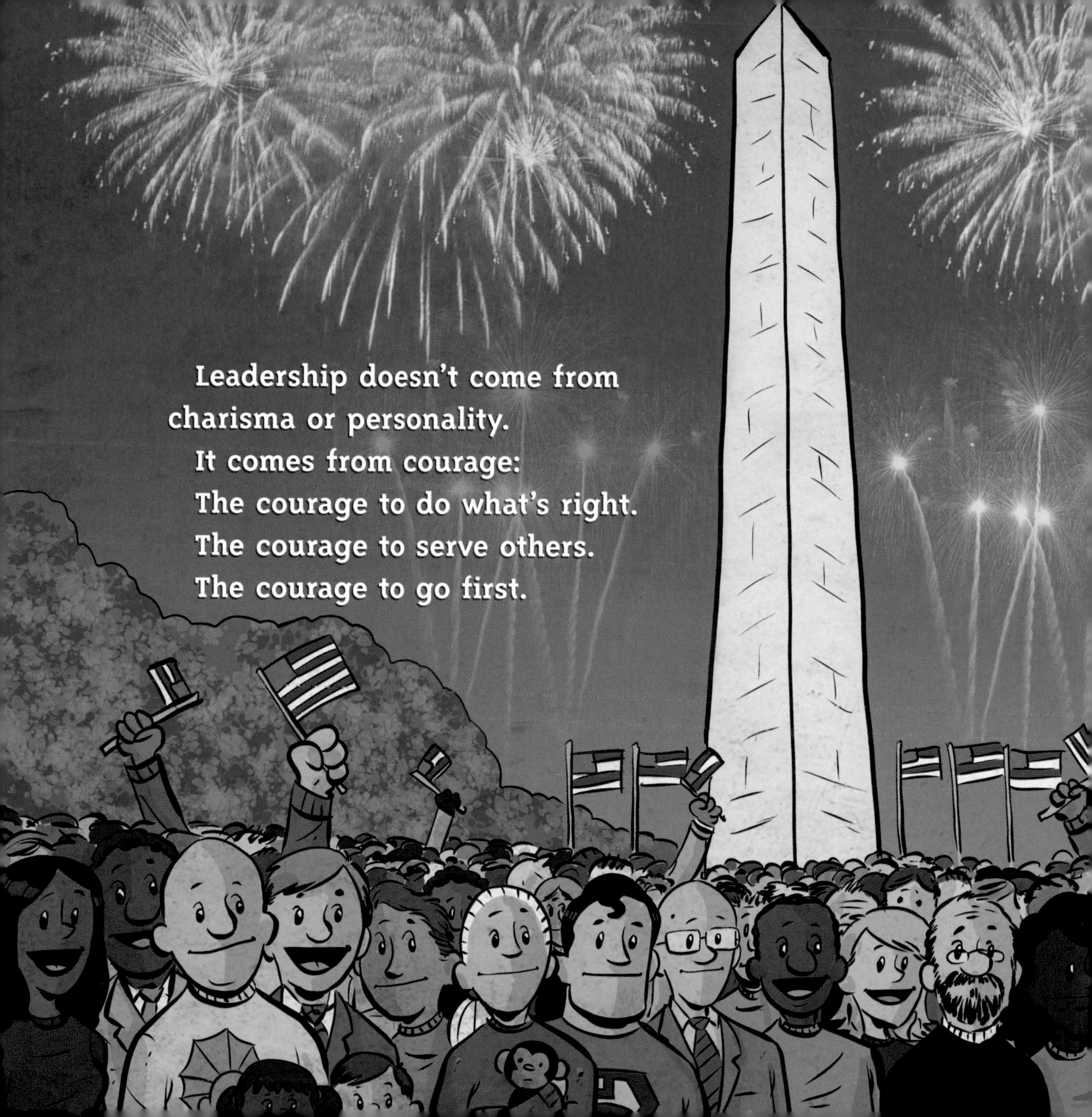

Leadership doesn't come from charisma or personality.

It comes from courage:

The courage to do what's right.

The courage to serve others.

The courage to go first.

I am George Washington.

Today they call me the father of our country.

I have the courage to do what no one's done before.

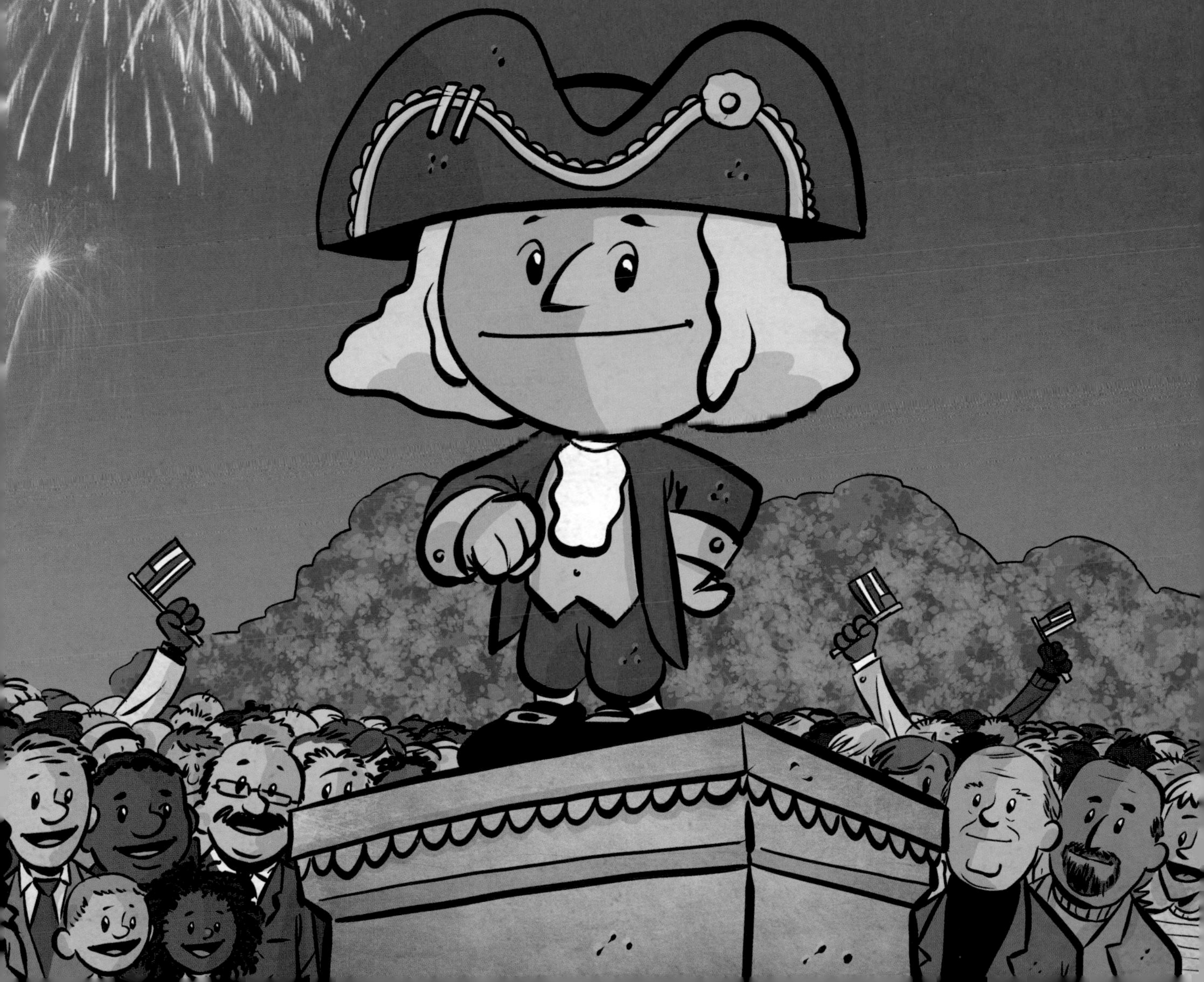

"I hope I shall always possess...virtue enough to maintain...the character of an honest man."
—George Washington

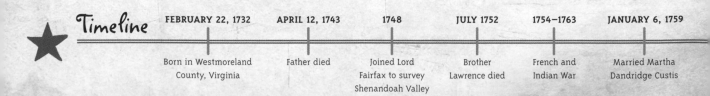

★ Timeline	FEBRUARY 22, 1732	APRIL 12, 1743	1748	JULY 1752	1754–1763	JANUARY 6, 1759
	Born in Westmoreland County, Virginia	Father died	Joined Lord Fairfax to survey Shenandoah Valley	Brother Lawrence died	French and Indian War	Married Martha Dandridge Custis

Mount Vernon,
George's home

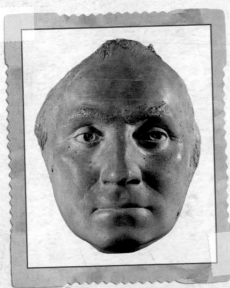

A mask of
George's face
upon his death

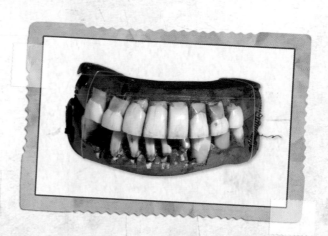

George's fake teeth
(gross, right?)

APRIL 1775	JUNE 15, 1775	DECEMBER 25–26, 1776	OCTOBER 19, 1781	APRIL 30, 1789	DECEMBER 14, 1799	1885
Battles of Lexington and Concord start American Revolution	Named Commander-in-Chief of Continental Army	Crossed the Delaware River	British surrender at Yorktown	Inaugurated as first U.S. President	Died at age 67 in Mount Vernon, Virginia	Presidents' Day established

For Eli Segal,
my first boss,
my first real job,
and the first to teach me about
the power of citizen service
and the impact of a great leader.
—B.M.

For Nate Cosby,
who put faith in me,
became my biggest cheerleader,
who pushed me to be a better artist,
but most of all, someone I consider family.
—C.E.

Special thanks to Joseph Ellis for his help and input.
Additional thanks to fearless leader Simon Sinek.

SOURCES
His Excellency: George Washington by Joseph J. Ellis (Vintage Books, 2004)
Washington: A Life by Ron Chernow (Penguin Press, 2010)
Washington: The Indispensable Man by James Thomas Flexner (Back Bay Books, 1994)
George Washington and Benedict Arnold: A Tale of Two Patriots by Dave R. Palmer (Regnery History, 2006)
Founding Father: Rediscovering George Washington by Richard Brookhiser (Free Press, 1996)

FURTHER READING FOR KIDS
Who Was George Washington? by Roberta Edwards (Grosset & Dunlap, 2009)
George Did It by Suzanne Tripp Jurmain (Dutton, 2005)
George Washington's Teeth by Deborah Chandra and Madeleine Comora (Farrar, Straus and Giroux, 2003)
The Founding Fathers!: Those Horse-Ridin', Fiddle-Playin', Book-Readin', Gun-Totin' Gentlemen
Who Started America by Jonah Winter (Atheneum, 2015)
Dear Mr. Washington by Lynn Cullen (Dial, 2015)

ROCKY POND BOOKS • An imprint of Penguin Random House LLC, New York

First published in the United States of America by Dial Books for Young Readers, an imprint of Penguin Random House LLC, 2016
This edition published by Rocky Pond Books, an imprint of Penguin Random House LLC, 2023

Text copyright © 2016 by Forty-four Steps, Inc. • Illustrations copyright © 2016 by Christopher Eliopoulos.

Portrait on page 38: Gilbert Stuart (American, 1755–1828), *George Washington*, 1796–1803. Sterling and Francine Clark Art Institute.
Photos on page 39: House and teeth, Courtesy of Mount Vernon Ladies' Association. Death mask, The Pierpont Morgan Library, New York.

Visit us online at PenguinRandomHouse.com.

Library of Congress Cataloging-in-Publication Data
Meltzer, Brad, author. • I am George Washington / Brad Meltzer ; illustrated by Christopher Eliopoulos. • pages cm. — (Ordinary people change the world) • Audience: Ages 5–8. • ISBN 978-0-525-42848-0 (hardcover) • 1. Washington, George, 1732–1799—Juvenile literature. 2. Presidents—United States—Biography—Juvenile literature. 3. Generals—United States—Biography—Juvenile literature. I. Eliopoulos, Chris, illustrator. II. Title. • E312.66.M447 2016 973.4'1092—dc23 [B] 2015036139

ISBN 9780525428480 | 13
Manufactured in China • Designed by Jason Henry • Text set in Triplex • The artwork for this book was created digitally.

This is a work of nonfiction. Some names and identifying details have been changed.
The publisher does not have any control over and does not assume any responsibility for author or third-party websites or their content.